AF512153

The Classics of
American Literature

From James Fenimore Cooper to J.P. Donleavy

R.K. Sharma

ATLANTIC

PUBLISHERS & DISTRIBUTORS (P) LTD

Published by
ATLANTIC
PUBLISHERS & DISTRIBUTORS (P) LTD
7/22, Ansari Road, Darya Ganj, New Delhi-110002
Phones : +91-11-40775252, 23273880, 23275880, 23280451
Fax : +91-11-23285873
Web : www.atlanticbooks.com
E-mail : orders@atlanticbooks.com

Branch Office
5, Nallathambi Street, Wallajah Road, Chennai-600002
Phones : +91-44-64611085, 32413319
E-mail : chennai@atlanticbooks.com

Copyright © R.K. Sharma, 2019

All rights reserved. No part of this publication may be reproduced, stored in a retrieval system, transmitted or utilized in any form or by any means, electronic, mechanical, photocopying, recording or otherwise, without the prior permission of the copyright owner. Application for such permission should be addressed to the publisher.

Disclaimer

The author and the publisher have taken every effort to the maximum of their skill, expertise and knowledge to provide correct material in the book. Even then if some mistakes persist in the content of the book, the publisher does not take responsibility for the same. The publisher shall have no liability to any person or entity with respect to any loss or damage caused, or alleged to have been caused directly or indirectly, by the information contained in this book.

The author has fully tried to follow the copyright law. However, if any work is found to be similar, it is unintentional and the same should not be used as defamatory or to file legal suit against the author.

If the readers find any mistakes, we shall be grateful to them for pointing out those to us so that they can be corrected in the next edition.

All disputes are subject to the jurisdiction of Delhi court only.

Printed in India at Nice Printing Press, A-33/3A, Site-IV, Industrial Area, Sahibabad, Ghaziabad, U.P.

Preface

The book includes articles, written at different times to be read out in seminars/conferences/classroom lecture-series with a view to demolishing certain misconceptions about a writer and his works that he propagates a bourgeois ideology or that his world view is shaped by the exaggerated concept of partisanship in art, and project his ideological commitments to a particular movement/school of thought in right prospective. Since the American writers have been alive to the contemporary European intellectual currents/movements, the print of which is reflected in showing their concerns with the predicament of man in a mass-mechanistic society, an attempt has been made to include articles which represent their characteristic world outlook and also with a view to becoming fully conversant with the evolution and history of the American theatre and the novel since the early times, when the Indian tribes, the Iroquois left the hunting ground to the white colonizers and moved to the West. As James Fenimore Cooper happens to be the first American novelist—a kind of frontierman of this phase of American expansionism—his one novel, *The Crater*, which is both "history and utopia" is included in the study, being critique of the American democracy, with the hopes for its regeneration.

It is also kept in mind that the articles be included, representing the five major trends which have injected a new vitality into Post-war American fiction since 1945, which Joseph J. Waldmeir on the basis of their inter-relatedness identifies as "the social critical", "the accommodationist", "the beat-absurd black humourist", "the quest" and "the neo-social critical". The critic, then proceeds to explain the reason why there was a shift from one to another trend, as partly wrought by historical necessity. The novels of social criticism, he shows, are the offshoot of the 'crusading' protest literature of the 1930s in which the social ills come under attack, such as poverty, exploitation, the problem of color and racism and the farm owners and their exploitative tendencies—John Steinbeck's *The Grapes of Wrath* (1939) being a case in point.

Marcus Klein uses the term, 'alienation' for the "social critical impulse", and he is right in the sense that the artist, in his critique of the system, is left an 'alien', despite all his social commitments to reform, and the more he is critical of the system, the more alienated he becomes. But the mode of social criticism provides a perspective which is that of accommodationism, and the novelists are designated as accommodationist who advocate for perfect harmony and understanding between the individual and the society, rather than support confrontation and antagonism: life, they see, despite all its odds and existential absurdity, in Camusian sense, worth-living.

The third trend is the 'quest-novel' which Waldmeir considers as the most significant in the American fiction since 1945, in terms of the "general critical acceptance". The war dislocated the elemental human values and left man to live with the 'scar'. As such, there began a quest in the midst of the growing feelings of senselessness and meaninglessness to affirm life to live by as it is. Prominent among them are the Jewish novelists such as Saul Bellow, Bernard Malamud, J.D. Salinger, John Updike, William Styron, and Norman Mailer. These writers find the approach for the traditional social criticism to the portrayal of reality and the anxieties of the time 'sterile'. They do not think that simple rejection or disaffiliation from the contemporary institutions that we see in the novels of black humor and the Beat literature, can assure a cogent and worthwhile strategy to fight out the evils of the time. This is the approach that has gone into the two articles—one on the Black Humor novelists, and the other on "The Beat Generation and J.P. Donleavy" wherein the vulgar and grotesque is satirized and the finer basic human values are affirmed in the line of the quest novelists, who, in response to their loss of faith in social criticism, seek "new bases of value and order".

And the fifth trend is "neo-social critical" in which the artists encounter a situation which is tragically paradoxical: they need love to transcend all differences—ideological, racial, color, economic—but what they see at the root is violence and terror continuing "to rip the cities". What happens in Ralph Ellison's *Invisible Man*? It is the visibility which comes first to affirm the individuality of a person—one cannot be loved unless one exists.

In the Victorian age, when a radical break was wrought by Darwin and other evolutionary scientists and there was a reconciliation between science and religion, popularly known as the "Victorian Compromise", it was felt that the golden age was round the corner, with widespread faith in the gradual advancement toward an era of perfect peace and prosperity. In America, this note of faith and confidence runs through the writings of Walt Whitman and R.W. Emerson, but by the time Eugene O'Neill took to writing, this dream had been shattered. The fruits of science and technology had turned to dust and frustration and disillusionment were widespread. *The Hairy Ape* is a fine expression of this spiritual and cultural decay in the West and the resultant disintegration of human personality in a highly technological and mechanized society, Yank being an entrapped ape in the stokehole.

One theme which has been haunting the American imagination is the dream of success. Plays and novels have been written wherein the "success-myth" and the "plantation-myth" are used as a backdrop to show the devastating impact of their illusory nature on man. Of various changes which took place in the post-war America, one was the introduction of television and the entry of the working class into the mass market for consumer durables and home ownership, who had long succumbed to the evils of consumerism and were destroyed during the process; the second was the pressure of the economic boom that created the mystique around the salesman—selling was taken as the greatest career a man could want. F. Scot Fitzgerald's *The Great Gatsby*—a novel of the Jazz-culture of the 20's—and Arthur Miller's *All My Sons* and *Death of a Salesman* capture this socio-economic and moral upheaval of the time.

Because the lead, as taken by the novels of social criticism, is best represented by the war-novels of World War II, the paper on "Anti-War American Novels" is included, not only to show that the novels under study are anti-war novels in the sense that they condemn war as metaphor of human suffering and thus instill in man's mind a hatred of war, but they are anti-war novels in another sense also, as M. Koreneva writes: they condemn the growth of the fascist tendencies in the army which threatened to spread from the army into the American society as a whole, for which they are designated as pro-war novels also, at the same time, they concede the necessity of war to fight a bigger enemy which is Fascism. James Jones shows his hero, Robert E. Lee Prewitt, being subjected to such dangerous reactionary tendencies, which are also reflected in Mailer's *The Naked and the Dead*, wherein General Cumming, the American, impresses upon Lieutenant Hearn's mind that war and politics are beyond morality—"the only morality of the future is a power morality".

The article on *The Scarlet Letter* examines Hester's moral position, as against the framework of the traditional Puritanism and salvation she seeks, as the Unitarians say, "by character, not by dogma," thereby questioning, for want of the absolutes, the inadequacy of the system. This is Hawthorne's humanism.

The novels, designated as classics, qualify a 'standard' as set forth by the ancients to call a work of art classic, which is that they not only tell a story or paint a pageant of colorful characters, but define man in a given situation to the effect that the account tends to become the criticism of life. If judged in this framework of value, *The Grapes of Wrath* is a class creation having a perennial appeal to go beyond place and time, notwithstanding that it has had its damming criticism since its publication (1939) in the areas which have been praised by the reviewers in the Oklahoma press, one is, for example, that it has been linked with the tradition of the naturalistic novels of the '30s for an honest and sympathetic treatment of the plight of the uprooted farmers of Oklahoma from the land. The clergy is also divided: one Reverend W. Lee Rector of Ardimore finds the book for its social protest "a heaven-shaming and Christ-insulting book", perhaps, partly for the unorthodox sermonizing of Jim Casy and his attitude to sexual morality and religion; a minister, on the contrary, is quoted to have it praised as a truthful book of literary as well as of social value "resembling in power and beauty of style King James' version of the Bible", which is sufficient to demolish the charge of vileness of language and factual inaccuracies.

Saul Bellow's *The Dean's December* is studied primarily for keeping the crucial question alive—how a good man should live—and having it finally settled, being closely drawn upon the philosophy of existential humanism and that of rebellion, Camus puts forth in *The Rebel*. Bellow's view of man is existential but his fascination for existentialism is as long as it does not tend to be nihilistic and has Christian flavor, the moment it turns atheistic, questioning God's existence, he parts company with the philosophers of existence, like Heidegger, Sartre and Camus, with the understanding that one cannot be good without God. Nonetheless, if he is drawn to Sartre, it is for his interpretation of man as 'project', that "man is nothing but that which he makes of himself", which is, though anti-Calvinist, yet it cannot be wholly downplayed in the context of what Ponge has written in a very fine article, "Man is the future of man". Sartre quotes in "Existentialism is a Humanism", "Man is all the time outside of himself: it is in projecting and losing himself beyond himself that he makes man exist." It is this transcending power of human consciousness Bellow is preoccupied with, and which has gone in the creation of heroes, which is reflected in their changing attitude to the contemporary post-war American reality, Alan Corde, the protagonist, being one fine extension of this principle of existence.

I hope the book will be of utmost value for the serious lovers of literature. It will stir in them the spirit of critical enquiry and inquisitiveness and help them to develop their own understanding of literature.

R.K. Sharma

Contents

Preface ... iii

1. James Fenimore Cooper's *The Crater*: 'A Parable of America' ... 1
2. Problems of Morality in Nathaniel Hawthorne's *The Scarlet Letter* ... 11
3. *The Great Gatsby*: A Critique of the American Dream of Success ... 24
4. Concept of Freedom: Henry James' *The Portrait of a Lady* ... 33
5. Existential Concerns in Eugene O'Neill's *The Hairy Ape* ... 44
6. Ontology in William Faulkner's *The Sound and the Fury* ... 55
7. Transcendence as Vision: A Study of Bernard Malamud's *The Assistant* ... 65
8. Treatment of Dream in Arthur Miller's *All My Sons* and *Death of a Salesman* ... 76
9. Feminist Concerns in Tennessee Williams's *A Streetcar Named Desire* ... 87
10. Anti-War American Novels ... 96

11. Contemporary Black Humour American Novels: From Nathanael West to Thomas Berger 112

12. Robert Frost's 'Birches'—An Appraisal.................... 124

13. The Beat Generation and James Patrick Donleavy 131

14. Humanism in John Steinbeck's *The Grapes of Wrath* 146

15. Saul Bellow's *The Dean's December*: 'Self as rebel' 157

Index 168

Chapter 1

James Fenimore Cooper's *The Crater*: 'A Parable of America'

"In Cooper", Robert E. Spiller writes, "the organic artist in America was born. He was the first writer of power to realize that a new literature must be created from the inside out, from the feeling to the form.... He was determined to put the whole of America, roots, and all, into his books."[1]

James Fenimore Cooper (1789-1851) was born in New Jersey, his father, William Cooper is a descendant of English Quakers, the family moved to their estate at Cooperstown on Otsego Lake, the Central New York which was still a frontier territory, where Cooper spent his boyhood. In many respects, as Spiller observes, he is the founding father of the novel in America, he wrote romances, historical and political novels and novels of manners and adventures on the sea, his novels (32 in number) are an authentic document of the history of American expansionism and the clash between wilderness and civilization. It is he who supplied the form and idea of the novel which was to take shape in the hands of the masters, like Hawthorne, Melville, Henry James, Mark Twain. His *Leather Stocking Tales*, which are the best group of novels, deal with the adventure of the frontier movement and the clash between the early settlers and the American Indians.

Cooper was a devoted republican. His humanistic ideals are reflected in his criticism of "all that he held most desirable in life", the freedom of thought, act and speech. He attacks the American democracy with a hope for its regeneration, the *Littlepage* novels Trilogy and *The Crater* are its powerful illustrations wherein he exhorts man to submit to the law of God and of human institutions.

The Crater is a sequel to the theme of social criticism, Cooper has dealt with in the Littlepage Trilogy;[2] written with a backdrop of the anti-rent struggle of the 1840s,[3] to warn people that what is essential for the survival of humanity is the moral sense and man's submission to the rule of God and of human institutions. Cooper saw in the struggle "the decay of a sense of values in the American mind", as Robert E. Spiller shows, he traces the decline of the New York landed aristocracy which, to him, "personified a lost ideal of democratic distinction in living."[4]

The novel is cast in an allegorical mode of narration, to show how man, far from the contemporary scene of class struggle, destroys himself and the social order which he builds around him after years' toils. The fact is illustrated by what happens to Mark Woolston and his islands which he establishes, by Divine Providence, in the Pacific Ocean, which Cooper writes, was not as much familiar to the navigators in 1796 as it is now. After the shipwreck of the American vessel, the Rancocus, Mark and his friend, Bob Betts survive, they plant vegetations in the volcanic ash of the island and intend to build a pinnace for return to America. But it so happens that Bob is lost (Ch. IX) in a tempest and Mark is left alone to move as Robinson Crusoe on the solitary island, "cut off from all communication with his kind," with nothing between him and God to commune with. As the history of Mark's establishment of the colony of the crater shows that much of Cooper's own experiences of Cooperstown and Robinson Crusoe[5] story has gone into the novel. A sudden earthquake raises a chain of islands above the water in which Mark sees the immense power and glory of God, revealed in nature; he finds himself alone as the possessor of a whole "new creation" like Adam in paradise and his wife Bridget as Eve, who later joined him with other friends. As the sole governor of the island, Mark sets on it an imaginary social organization, based on the moral principles, derived from his own training, intellect and education. In the creation of Mark, Cooper, consciously or unconsciously; draws upon Plato's idea of a 'philosopher ruler' that one who rules should be knowledgeable and good. The argument as advanced by Dixon Ryan Fox about the philosophy of the Federalist Party hardly betrays any iota of partisan bias.

> They believed that the government by the wise and the good was better than by the ignorant and vicious. But a larger portion of the wise and the good was to be found among the men of property than among society at large. Those who had it by inheritance had therefore more of leisure to acquire wisdom and work and were immune from the passion of cupidity, while those who earned it did so by the exercise of those abilities which might be serviceable to the state, ergo, government by the part was preferable to government by the whole.[6]

What Dixon thinks of the vices which destroy the goodness of the common man more easily than of aristocracy goes in the creation of Mark Woolston. Mark is that individual who has in mind the idea to plant an ideal community on the island, presuming the island to be the mythical Eden and the inhabitants as innocent as Adam, uncorrupted by evil, to ascertain the truth of man whether evil lies within him or in the system and what happens when man seeks divorce from the original source to be more than human.

Thomas Philbrik in the Introduction to *The Crater* shows the impact of Fourier's socialist theories "on Cooper which is reflected in Mark's planning of a more sensible, hence more durable utopian community", keeping in view the issue of equality, property and dignity of labour; whether the community or the individual labour is ideal? Mark, Cooper writes, is an individual who is alive to the value of the dignity of labour. Some among his imaginary population favour the idea of shared property and community labour which Mark does not support, rather he makes sure that each family has a private piece of ground, which even escaped the eye of the Founding Fathers, and which is in contravention of his earlier view of landlord system.

> Mark Woolston was much too sensible a man to fall into any of the modern absurdities on the subject of equality,

> and a community of interest. One or two individuals, even in that day, had wished to accompany him, who were for forming an association in which all property should be shared in common, and in which nothing was to be done but that which was right. Mark had not the least objection in the world to the last proposition, and would have been glad enough to see it carried out to the letter, though he differed essentially with the applicants, as to the mode of achieving so desirable an end. He was of opinion that civilization could not exist without property, or property without a direct personal interest in both its accumulation and its preservation.[7]

Mark does not support the idea of the community labour that "a hundred men would be happier and better off with their individualities compressed into one, than by leaving them in a hundred subdivisions, as they had been placed by nature."[8] The theory is flawed because the hundred individuals cannot be compressed into one, it is a 'riot'.

The colony reaches a point when it is felt that certain great principles be established, the governor did not relish powers for power's sake but only wielded for the general good. It was now quite a "gem in the way of vegetation." Cooper describes its Edenesque purity:

> The visitation terminated at the peak. The place aptly likened to the garden of Eden, and frequently so called, could receive very little addition to its picturesque beauties from the hand of man. Parts of it were cultivated, it is true; enough to supply its population (rather more than three hundred souls) with food; but much the greater portion of its surface was in pasture.... Everything false was carefully avoided, and, with no great pretensions in the way of acquisitions, the schools of the Peak were made to be useful, and at least innocent. One thing the governor strictly enjoined; and that was, to teach these young creatures that they were fallible beings, carefully avoiding the modern fallacy of supposing that an infallible whole could be formed of fallible parts.[9]

Yet the governor and his wife are not aware of the fact that "the serpent of old was about to visit this Eden of modern times."[10] The devil in the form of a "professor" once again entered Eden; and the Peak, with so much to raise the soul above the grosser strife of men, was soon ringing with discussions on "free grace," "immersion," "spiritual baptism," and the "apostolical succession."[11] The healthful humility of the human being is infected by two dangers—the 'luxurious idleness', and "waxing fat and kicking."[12] Besides, an exaggerated view of self and an almost total forgetfulness of God, overtook the colonial humility and the three agents to heighten this view of self are—"religion, law and the press."[13] Religion cuts deeper in human consciousness, the Press, Cooper calls humorously the "Crater Truth-Teller", advanced a theory of the power of majority that it "had the right to do as it pleased,"[14] being unaware of the dangers, lurking underneath, as the governor stated in several communications himself, that "if a majority has a right to rule, in this arbitrary manner, it has a right to set its dogmas above the Commandments, and to legalize theft, murder, adultery, and all the other sins denounced in the twentieth chapter of Exodus;" and "that the laws of God which he allowed that even majorities were bound to respect. There upon, the governor replied that the laws of God were nothing but the great principles which ought to govern human conduct, and that his concession was an avowal that there was a power to which majorities should defer."[15] Cooper writes:

> There was a great deal of good sense, and much truth in what the governor wrote, on this occasion; but of what avail could it prove with the ignorant and short-sighted, who put more trust in one honeyed phrase of the journal, that flourished about the 'people' and their 'rights', than in all the arguments that reason, sustained even by revelation, could offer to show the fallacies and dangers of this new doctrine.

A convention was held, fortified by the sacred principle of the sway of majority and new laws were drawn for the election. And Mark as governor, they feared, could still command more votes for the office than any other man in the colony, they brought one article to keep him out of power that no person should hold the office of the governor more than five years consecutively. Thus by cunning they placed the governor "on the shelf at the next election."[16] Election followed the adoption of the new constitution, a farmer John Pennock, was chosen governor for two years, the new lawyer was made the judge, the editor, secretary of the state and treasurer; committees were nominated to lay all the Woolston connection completely on the shelf which placed the power in the hands of a few in a government of the many. Cooper's dig at the rule of the majority is apparent that "it is so sacred a thing that it is found necessary to regulate it by legerdemain. No good republican ever disputes the principle, while no sagacious ever submits to it."[17]

Thus, a great revolution effected in the colony of the crater. Mark submitted to the changes and ceased to be anything more than a private citizen. But what he watches thereafter by the progress of events is all a dismal story; he has learnt a truth—a political truth—which the author has summed up in capital letters.

> THAT THE MORE A PEOPLE ATTEMPT TO EXTEND THEIR POWER DIRECTLY OVER STATE AFFAIRS, THE LESS THEY, IN FACT, CONTROL THEM, AFTER HAVING ONCE PASSED THE POINT OF NAMING LAWGIVERS AS THEIR REPRESENTATIVES MERELY BESTOWING ON A FEW ARTFUL MANAGERS THE INFLUENCE THEY VAINLY IMAGINE TO HAVE SECURED TO THEMSELVES.[18]

As the two elder children are to be sent to Pennsylvania for education, Bridget expresses a strong wish to visit America once more. Mark, being much mortified at the turn things had taken, agrees to go back from the Peak. Thus sailing on the Rancocus, the Woolston reach the little town of Bristol.

Now the interest shifts on what happens during Mark's absence on the Crater: the morals decayed with religion obtaining false direction, the merchants behaved badly in the political struggle, verging on the intense selfishness and the caste-hierarchy in the pursuit of gain, the good population was converted into a mobocracy.

What is disheartening is what Mark finds on his revisitation of the sight where there once existed a colony of his town plantation. On his departure he left it surrounded with a sort of earthly paradise and found, it on return, all buried beneath the ocean. He could behold nothing but the summit of the Peak and the solitary tree as a signal, signifying the truth of man—how hard it is to shed evil! But little was told about the colony of the crater and its fortunes by its survivors. Cooper writes addressing sea, symbolic of God's power:

> This is thy lesson, mighty sea! Man calls the dimpled earth his own. The flowery vale, the golden lea; And on the wild gray mountain-stone claims nature's temple for his throne! But where thy many voices sing. Their endless song, the deep, deep tone calls back his spirit's airy wing. He shrinks into himself, when God is king![19]

Mark and Bridget ponder deep over the changes and the manner in which the colony came into existence which was most extraordinary and went out of it in one that was awful: all this was to colour and chasten their future life.

Mark fails to reconcile why the ministers, the editors and the demagogues indulged in irresponsible activities that led to the disappearance of the colony, a God's bounty to man. Who are responsible for the disaster? Certainly, there is no gods' hand, the agents are human agents, to act out as 'despoiler'. It is men who because of "their fallen nature violate the clearest laws of God and men, they are ejected or destroyed, the new Eden disappear, leaving a mankind more or less where it was."[20] It is the islanders who have made hell of heaven; freedom, if put to disuse, takes man back to a state of primitive savagery.

The island is the very image of America, in the early phase of colonization, it was God's Garden bestowed upon men to use, not to put to disuse. The disaster is God's judgment upon a wanton and wayward society that ceased to have faith in the principle and were lost in the melee of the feverish pursuits of amoral materialism. The novel is thus a 'parable of America' which once was a paradise. The government before the decay of the crater island, stood 'on moral foundations but perished later when they were flouted. What of contemporary America? Cooper seems to warn the Americans that the contemporary society could fall like Mark's establishment for want of some sound moral principles to stand on.

There are some who see exaggeration in Cooper's account of decay of Mark's imaginary community. George Dekker being one for example, to whom "the account of the social and political decline of the island community is absurdly perfunctory—an allegorical caricature of the decline of the American republic.[21]

Cooper's analysis of the genesis of the disaster of the colony of the crater is not utopian; so long as the colony pursued the right, it existed, and when it began to pursue the wrong, it perished. What is true of the colony is true of the human world and its much coveted advantages. Cooper's Episcopalian fervor sees the seeds of decay in man's anthropocentric world view when the self replaces the 'divine', thereby ironically incur Being's spiritual enfeeblement and loss of self-esteem.

> For a time our efforts seem to create, and to adorn, and to perfect, until we forget our origin and destination, substituting self for that divine hand which alone can unite the elements of worlds as they float in gases, equally from His mysterious laboratory, and scatter them again into thin air when—the works of his hand cease to find favour in His view.[22]

However, the novel ends with a moral, exhorting man never to forget his 'littleness', as against the vast immensity of God, as revealed in nature.

> Let those who would substitute the voice of the created for that of the Creator, who shout "the people, the people," instead of hymning the praises of their God, who vainly imagine that the masses are sufficient for all things, remember their insignificance and tremble. They are but mites amid millions of other mites, that the goodness of providence has produced for its own wise ends; their boasted countries with their vaunted climates and production, have temporary possessions of but small portions of a globe that floats, a point, in

> space. Following the course pointed out by an invisible finger, and which will one day be suddenly struck out of its orbit, as it was originally put there, by the hand that made it. Let that dread Being, then, be never made to act a second part in human affairs, or the rebellious vanity of our race imagine that either numbers, or capacity, or success, or power in arms, is aught more than a short-lived gift of His beneficence, to be resumed when His purposes are accomplished.[23]

Thus by dramatizing the reversal of fortunes of the colony of the crater and its community in the last two chapters (Ch. 29-30), Cooper stressed the need of realisation of divinity in man which is essential for the survival of humanity. His Episcopalian faith and humanistic ideals have gone in the making of *The Crater* which is read as a class creation in island literature with so simple a moral.

Notes

1. Robert E. Spiller, *The Cycle of American Literature: An Essay in Historical Criticism*, A Mentor Book, New York, The New American Library, 1956, p. 44.
2. The three novels of the Littlepage Triology are *Satanstoe* (1845), *The Chainbreaker* (1845) and *The Redskins* (1846).
3. A vast stretch of land was let on leases to the tenants in New York State who wanted it to be sold out to them on their own terms which the landlords refused. A hostility broke out between the two classes against this so-called "feudal system" which degenerated to the point of war, the seeds of which were sown since the colonial times.
4. *The Cycle of American Literature: An Essay in Historical Criticism, op. cit.*, p. 44.
5. W.B. Gates, "A Note on Cooper and Robinson Crusoe", *Modern Language Notes*, 1952, Vol. LXVII, pp. 421-22.
6. Dixon Ryan Fox, *The Decline of Aristocracy in the Politics of New York: 1801-1840* (Rpt.), New York Harper Torch Books, 1965, p. 249.
7. James Fenimore Cooper, *The Crater*, The Project Gutenberg e-Book, 2004, p. 101.
8. *Idem.*

9. *Ibid.*, p. 130.
10. *Ibid.*, p. 132.
11. *Ibid.*, p. 146.
12. *Ibid.*, p. 145.
13. *Idem.*
14. *Ibid.*, p. 147.
15. *Ibid.*, pp. 147-48.
16. *Ibid.*, p. 149.
17. *Idem.*
18. *Ibid.*, p. 150.
19. *Idem.*
20. George Dekker, *James Fenimore Cooper: The American Scott,* New York, Barnes and Noble Inc., 1967, p. 248.
21. *Ibid.*, p. 158.
22. *The Crater*, p. 155.
23. *Idem.*

Chapter 2

Problems of Morality in Nathaniel Hawthorne's *The Scarlet Letter*

Hawthorne's *The Scarlet Letter* is, in his own words, "a tale of human frailty and sorrow" but much dust is raised over the problems of morality, sin and salvation in the wake of the shifting cultural and moral pattern of man-woman relationship in New England history. A classroom lecture on the novel leaves a student often with a disturbing query in regard to Hester's moral position and Hawthorne's defence of it. What of Hester's sin? If she is not a sinner, what is she then? What is the explanation of what she says to the persistent query of Pearl about the significance of the letter 'A' that it is the mark of the Black Man, she met "once in my life time?", or that "she knew that her deed had been evil, she had no faith, therefore, that its result (Pearl) would be good?" This is tantamount to the confession of sin but the manner in which she interprets her sin after seven years in the forest private meeting to Arthur that her adultery "had a consecration of its own" makes her position ambiguous. And whether the ambiguity is by design, or it is so by its very nature of the theme Hawthorne has chosen to deal with, is the real dialectic, the novel is constructed on.

The truth is that Hester Prynne from the first, in the words of John C. Cerber, "does not consider her act of adultery as a sin against God or against any law of her own nature. Nor does she feel that she has sinned against the community. Yet clearly she knows that her deed has been wrong and that, somehow, the result cannot be good." The word "somehow" is intriguing but

Seymour Gross has brilliantly turned its logic toward Hester's defence stating that "she cannot imagine any law as taking precedence over the law of love between a man and a woman."[1] But it is not Godwinism[2] that has influenced her concept of marriage: marriage as she understands, is a sacramental union only when there is love to truly sacramentalize it. She is linked twice with Anne Hutchinson in the story to show that like her, she is convinced through "inner light", that her way is not a violation of God's law. This is what she means in the "Conclusion" when she tells the women who come to seek her counsel:

> She assured them, too, of her firm belief, that, at some brighter period, when the world should have grown ripe for it, in Heaven's own time, a new truth would be revealed, in order to establish the whole relation between man and woman on a surer ground of mutual happiness.[3]

Hester's prophetic idea of 'a new truth' about man-woman relationship and 'mutual happiness' does not in any way denigrate her as a case of irresponsible libertine. Nor has the novelist wished, as Seymour Gross points out, to portray her as a seventeenth century Sadie Thompson[4] or Anatole France's Thais[5] to pervert Arthur Dimmesdale's attempted escape from the spiritual tormentation and despair and misery. It is on the contrary a doctrine to enrich our human experience and humanize our responses to its inadequacies. Equally, her romantic individualism is not a gesture of posing her will against the will of God either as some critics have maintained while bracketing her with the two most God-rejecters, Ahab of the Pequod (*Moby Dick*) and Ivan Karamajov (*The Brothers Karamajov*). The forest scene is a further debasement which is prompted by the minister's sense of defeat, not by Hester's guile. The language Hester speaks when he begs her to resolve for him and advise what to do is hardly the language of a woman who is accused of "desperate recklessness" and "unyokable paganism".

> "You wrong yourself in this," said Hester, gently. "You have deeply and sorely repented. Your sin is left behind you, in the days long past. Your present life is not less holy, in very truth, than it seems in people's eyes. Is there

> no reality in the penitence thus sealed and witnessed by good works? And wherefore should it not bring you peace?"[6]

Let us be more precise about Hester's moral position and the milieu she is planted to reflect its moral ambivalence. There are three possible approaches to Hester's sin. The traditional answer to the question—is the act symbolised by the scarlet letter sinful—is a "Yes" because Hester has certainly violated the text of the Commandments. Second, the romantics hold the forces of social determinism responsible for the moral disaster and defend Hester on point of being true to "the deepest human instincts." Third, the transcendental idealists aver that Hester did not sin against what she thought was moral, she believed in a higher law which is the law of "the new morality of nature and the human heart." But her playing deception to protect her lover, during the interrogation in the first pillory-scene, they hold, is a sin both against her own 'integrity' and against God and if she had told everything in the beginning she would have been "blameless." But, then one can say, that there would have been no novel which is also true. But Hawthorne's position is otherwise different; the logic he puts forth in the book looks ambiguous to those who fail to understand his attitude to sin and morality. As a matter of fact, what is at the centre of the story is the transformation of the two sinners—Hester and Dimmesdale. Surprisingly enough, Hester is accused of raising a scandal in "godly Master Dimmesdale's Church", who himself is the serpent to devour her Edenesque purity, but the process of regeneration is self-contradictory whereas the truth of the two, being the same; is known to them alone. In case of Hester, it is social in that in the eyes of men the sinner becomes the saint with no confession in the traditional sense. The truth is that it is not the miracle of the 'scarlet letter' that has transformed the 'scarlet woman' into a 'Sister of Mercy' and 'the light of the sick room' but it is Hester's sacrifice and suffering which has effected the change of heart, essential for the swing from good to evil and evil to good and which has no laws to operate in that the same man who happens to be a Christ may turn out to be a Judas any time. Hester could have easily run away to be obscure into the unfamiliar darkness of the forest but she chooses "the scene of her guilt" as "the scene of her earthly punishment" which is a sure sign of her uncorrupted conscience and innocence.

Hester's knowledge of the scriptures is very scanty, as compared to Arthur's but a rich reservoir of humanity is her strength with which she settles in a milieu that is sceptical of female virtue without ever being sure of its own. One of the five statements of faith of the Unitarians is of "salvation by character, not by dogma" and therefore, if salvation is exoneration from the stigma, then Hester's self arrives at illumination by rising above the mundane nature of reality and is regenerated. In the other, as the Puritans have it, it is spiritual, but the various interpretations of the letter 'A' on the minister's breast by the gullible spectators make things ambiguous and romantic: the truth seems to be not what it is, but what it is taken to be.

However, a look into the historical context and the sources of the story will help us to understand better the genesis of Hester and her placement in a traditional Christian society. Hawthorne has largely drawn upon Caleb H. Snow's *History of Boston* and Joseph B. Felt's *Annals of Boston*. In Felt, there is no reference of Hester Pryne and therefore, the "real" Hester is largely "a fabrication", relocated by Hawthorne's imagination.[7] The Salem Quarterly Court, convened in November 1668 recorded the story of a woman of Duxbury town of Plymouth who was subjected to whipping for moral lapses, and the manner in which the entire case was conducted provided Hawthorne opportunities to carpenter the story of a woman who was first led morally astrayed by a priest and was later branded as an adulterous, leaving much to our amazement, her co-sinner unpunished. This doubleness of moral standards evidently nettled Hawthorne's Puritanism and *The Scarlet Letter* is an attempt to bring out the relevance of moral postulates of Puritanism.

The novel begins with Hester, being brought out of the prison to make her stand on the pillory in the market and show her sin to the (pious?) Puritans. There she encounters her husband Roger Chillingworth after two years which is tragic and adds mystery and awe to make the story gloomier and blighted. As per ritual, Hester is questioned by the Elders of the Church to name the sinner, to "give your child a father" but she refuses to do so. How to interpret her refusal? It is so because she, as a rebel, has begun to understand the mechanics of the age-long pattern of man-woman relationship, as nurtured and sanctified by the patriarchs? Or it is Hawthorne himself who does not *permit* her to do so, fearing that naming the co-sinner would put a stop to the thesis of the novel? The truth is that despite his denigration, he does not look upon her fall so grievous a moral sin, on way to realize the American dream of freedom, as the Puritans do. The silence is a weapon, fit to hit at the base of the system which encourages women-oppression, and partly to evolve her own strategy of survival to somehow live by. She is then taken back to the prison where Roger, as a physician, enters to cure her sick child. The confrontation is dramatic. What is revealed is painful in that her separation, though a co-incidence, turns out to be a case of loveless marriage. Hester says, "Thou knowst that I was frank with thee. I felt no love, nor feigned any", which Roger unhesitatingly acquiesces to be true and realizes his folly and frigidity responsible for the break-up of marriage.

> "I have greatly wronged thee," murmured Hester. "We have wronged each other," answered he. "Mine was the first wrong, when I betrayed thy budding youth into a false and unnatural relation with my decay."[8]

Roger fails to persuade his wife to reveal the identity of the co-sinner but succeeds in making her swear not to reveal his identity too. These details, comprising four chapters, are a prelude to the story and thereafter it is all Hawthorne's architectonic sense to handle and examine the wisdom of the Christian dogmas if they really help a sinner. This comes into clash with his own humanism when he calls Arthur's penitence a mockery of the idea of the spiritual purity in the second pillory scene. The locale, Roger tells Hester in the Interview-Scene, is the "wild outskirt of the earth," which is enough to prognosticate her tragedy. With the badge of sin blazing on her gown. Hester moves as an outsider in the colony.

Seven years are elapsed, the universe changes and during the process of moral progression, not repentance (as she does not consider her sin to be so), the sinful woman becomes "our Hester, the town's own Hester—who is so kind to the poor, so hopeful to the sick, so comfortable to the afflicted." In the eyes of the Boston community, Hester herself assumes something of a saintly character: the ignominious letter which "had the effect of the cross on a nun's bosom", imparted to her "a kind of sacredness" and gave her the look of "a personage of high dignity among her people." What Hawthorne further tells is not wholly romance but something to heighten reality that an Indian had drawn his arrow against the badge and the missile having struck it "fell harmless to the ground." Such reactions amply substantiate what W.C. Browell observes that the novel is "not a story of adultery but what David Stouck rightly points out that it is the novelist's judgement passed "only on the community as a whole—on its prejudices, and on its actions."

Hester has both her critics and apologists. Her tragedy is the result of the conflicting moralities in action: the orthodox morality of the minister confronts her own transcendental morality. The traditional moralists hold her truly a sinful woman, they see in her the image of the rejecter of the authority of God and of society. The recent critics, prominent among them are John Erskine, Darrel Abel, Stuart P. Sherman, Frederick I. Carpenter, have defended Hester's romantic self-indulgence on the plea that she is true to nature which is the moral heart of the novel that Hawthorne wishes to impress upon us: "Be true! Be true!...show freely to the world is not your worst, yet some trait whereby the worst may be inferred."[9] Sherman sees her "a free spirit liberated in a moral wilderness." Erskine finds little in the story to suggest that Hester's stepping out of moral order was sinful, "the passion itself...was sacred and never caused them repentance." Darrel Abel sees her a case of "more sinned against than sinning." If feminism evokes the idea of dependence syndrome, Richard Harter Fogle looks upon her as "a great early feminist," for freeing herself from any dependence upon the laws of puritan society, an another Hutchinson, the foundress of a religious sect";[10] Frederick I. Carpenter sees Hester's rise of trust in the belief of possibility of a new morality in the new world who "achieved spiritual greatness in spite of her own human weakness, in spite of the prejudices of her Puritan society and finally, in spite of the prejudices of her creator himself."[11]

The Puritan society under its institutional aspect, not society as collective humanity, has done more damage than as an individual to Hester: she could not escape the wrath of its guillotine. But the fumes of conflict between the individual, seeking fulfillment and the society working as an inimical force to thwart those aspirations, Prof. Carpenter feels, will never evaporate. Hester's tragedy "would still be the same in every century. It would result from her own deception and from the conflicting moral belief of her lover. But it would not result from her own sense of guilt or shame."[12]

How to live then with the scar of sin is Hawthorne's primary concern and his position in this regard is less dubious and vexing. He is not a dogmatist. And if the confusion is created by the mode of symbolism or partly by his own interpretation of the puritan dogma as way of life, it is born of the clash between his humanism and the ingrained tradition of Puritanism he inherited which is reflected in the changing pattern of the scarlet-letter symbology suggesting that though, the novelist's concern is with the Original Sin everywhere, yet his warfare is not with the innateness of sin in man but with its mode of transcendence and the manner in which the sinner is punished by the Puritan rulers with the conviction that the fall of guillotine would transform a picaro into a saint. He is not against the wisdom of the Commandments, but he is certainly against the enforced confession and the "unpardonable" Puritan practice of exposure of sin with no moral direction to live with sin. Hawthorne proceeds with the vision of an existential humanist to anatomize the weakness and the strength of human spirit, connecting it with the central motif of sin of adultery which is washed out by character, not dogma.

There are three sinners—Hester is guilty of the sin of sexuality and the sentence inflicted on her person is, in the eyes of Roger, "a wise sentence" which could be moral from the standpoint of a wronged husband; Roger's sin is the sin of intellectual hatred, the sin of self-consuming revenge which Hawthorne says, is a sin against "the sanctity of human heart."[13] But because it has transformed a man, who nine years ago was so "thoughtful for others, craving little for himself", into a fiend, and it is for this fiendish metamorphosis and loss of humanity that he holds Hester as much responsible as he does Arthur:

> "Who made me so?"
>
> "It was myself!;" cried Hester, shuddering. "It was, I, not less than he. Why hast thou not avenged thyself on me?"
>
> "I have left thee to the scarlet letter," replied Roger Chillingworth. "If that have not avenged me, I can do not more!"[14]

Roger, one can say, is a victim of man's inhumanity to man and the patriarchal puritan rigidity. But is his self-styled strategy the right answer to setting things right which has no moral sanction? He is well aware of his own role in Hester's tragedy and his realisation is rooted in the humanists' belief that it is love, reciprocity, involvement and understanding that bind man and woman into togetherness and marital fidelity. If he had taken a little care of Hester's youth and beauty, she could have been saved from the serpent's sting and the resultant betrayal, deceit, moral hypocrisy and treachery of the Boston society. The "polluted" pastor-paramour, Arthur, is the third sinner. His sin is the sin of concealment and moral hypocrisy for which Roger wants to have him hurled from the pulpit to the gallows and for which he has the author's sympathy. His sin is of moral falsity, he is not 'true' to nature and that is why his mechanical placement of hand on his heart has not disciplined him to 'truth' the way the scarlet letter has done Hester. It is the pride and the social facade and the fear of being divested of the trappings which deter him from open confession. Hawthorne's portrayal of Hester's moral triumph against the dismal picturisation of the Boston village population in all its ruthlessness, bereft of Christian virtues, such as love compassion, mercy, supports the contention that Hester is not a sinner and the sin of adultery she is held guilty of, is not so grievous a sin in the eyes of the ethical humanists. There are more important concerns than sexual lapses, such as "cruelty, greed, intolerance, slander, untrustworthiness"[15] which men perpetrate on women for the satisfaction of male-pride, forgetting the basic principle of ethical humanism that the individual happiness without advancing that of others is not virtue but "masochism."

In the existing situation the quality of moral life, the individual lives by, should not to be measured by the worn-out, narrow dogmatic framework of morality. Morality, if dictated by male-chauvinistic machinery, tends to be dubious and vitiating to the growth of human values. To be moral is to be human which urges upon us to accept man as he is in moments of spiritual triumphs and defeats. The Puritan establishment has been harsh to deal with Hester's guilt. Society has heard her story and has done the worst. But can the society know the truth (known to her alone) which she carries within her heart? The portrayal of the crowd, the discussion of a group of women about the leniency of the punishment awarded to Hester and the manner in which the beadle conducts her to the pillory, driving her like a mute animal as if her touch were moral pollution, make the mockery of the whole system. Hester repels the beadle by an action, marked with natural dignity and force of character. She steps into the open air as if by her own free will. What is the secret of this extra strength and boldness—Hawthorne's sympathy or her own understanding of the guilt which she feels is no guilt at all? It may be either but the paradox it involves is painful in that we feel relieved to see Hester freed from sin in the absence of the absolute moral standards but, at the same time, we rejoice to see the clergy catch Hester in the streets and use 'the scarlet letter' as an aid to teach the alphabets of morality to the ignorant Puritans. And the comicality is that we cannot have both together at the same time. This is the tragic dilemma which is at the heart of the novel and which, if misconstrued, will distort its very intended meaning. And it is in this context that we have to examine Hester's sin from the standpoint of the Boston community and of a new version of it as advocated by the novelist.

Hawthorne has to rationalise another problem involving "free will" that has its own morality to characterise the resultant good and evil. Values are deduced from the conditions of living which includes the acceptance of the limits of the possible. And if the individual chooses to lead an honest life of moral obligation and accountability, the act is moral. Keeping this view of man, Hawthorne's portrayal of Hester may for sometime tense the Puritan eye-brows but the tension is diffused the moment when one becomes conscious of the movements of the novel. It is by her own 'free will' that Hester sinned. It is by her own choice that she chooses to make the place of sin the place of her penance and suffering. She could not escape this predicament if she so willed otherwise. How is it that in the eyes of Hawthorne, Hester with "a burning blush and yet a haughty smile"[16] still looks more lady-like? The sight is painful for a sensitive observer. The burning letter, so blazing ón her bosom, has the effect of a spell, taking her out of the ordinary relation with humanity. The crowd's reaction to the sight at the pillory, which is of "smile instead of awe and shudder,"[17] is a display of moral darkness and makes the travesty of the whole show. It is further redeemed by what Hawthorne sees in Hester:

> Had there been a Papist among the crowd of the Puritans, he might have seen in this beautiful woman, so picturesque in her attire and mien and with the infant at her bosom, an object to remind him of the image of Divine Maternity, which so many illustrious painters have vied with one another to represent something which should remind him, indeed but only by contrast of that sacred image of sinless motherhood, whose infant was to redeem the world.[18]

The Calvinistic theology proclaims man's total depravity and his inability to work out salvation by himself. What does then the raising of Hester's purity to the level of Divine Maternity signify? To say that it is condonation rather than condemnation of sin is hardly convincing. Hawthorne sees the whole case from the standpoint of a man of flesh and blood. The portrayal of purity finds support in the dying words of Arthur, that "in view of Infinite Purity we are sinners all alike."[19] It is an honest admission of human imperfections but mighty and mournful. Hester is not in the dark about her sin and its possible transcendence within human limitations. This is the moral scale of the novelist to measure one's humanness which Hester alone seems to have learnt in the colony of Plymouth. That is why he does not view Hester as a sinner the way the New World sees it. The scarlet letter 'A' has been rightly condemned as a weapon of "red-hot brand of Puritanism" and its wisdom is not unequivocal for the reason that the users themselves become oblivious of its incipient bite end ironically accept the change in its character.

Richard Chase has rightly pointed out that in the understanding of Puritanism, Hawthorne finds him alone, no one to share his humanistic attitude to man's fallibility. Hence, the clash of attitudes to sin and salvation which is the strength of the book. To Roger, Hester is a tragic character in whom much good is wasted for want of strength to overcome evil. She makes a plea to him to spare Arthur and purge himself of evil to be once more human but it fails to move him. The physician is willing to pity her, not her lover "for the good that has been wasted in thy nature." This shows that Roger, like Hawthorne is also aware of human imperfections and innateness of sin: anyone can fall to the level of bestiality and thus his condonation of Hester's sin is not blasphemy but a human gesture. His sympathetic attitude to Hester's sin and of hatred and revenge towards that of Arthur has its own morality of seeking fulfilment. The sense of wrong done to him by a man of pulpit has perverted his intellect. The good, he thinks, is to unmask hypocrisy, rather than letting it prosper in privacy.

The view, therefore, that salvation is impossible, is demolished in the affirmation of the sacred in man existing with the sinful: man can be small, wretched, sensual, miserable, acquisitive but not mean. He has the capacity to make good of evil by keeping restraint over his overriding passion, vanity and egotism. But will putting the sinner to public humiliation and ridicule do any good to the sinner or to the system, if human thought and imagination has not been able to jettison the dismal severity of the puritanic code of law? As a matter of truth, the position which Hester's humanity has earned is very much near to in purity, as any ecclesiastical authority is supposed to be endowed with. She has thus "like all tragic protagonists demonstrated the dignity and potentialities of man even in her defeat" and this brings us closer to Hawthorne's humanism. The idea behind the forced addition of the ignominious scarlet letter to her dress is the recognition of her guilt for the satisfaction of the Boston Puritan crowd or even to tell the ordinary men that some moral order is transgressed which is a truth of the sacrament and which Hawthorne too does not contradict. Yet his thesis is too simplistic: moral values must be decontextualised from the mantle of theological dogma and the moral ideals must be constantly re-examined and revised in the light of the present needs and social demands.

Notes

1. Seymour Gross, "Form and Content in *The Scarlet Letter*," *The New England Quarterly*, 17, 1944, p. 359.
2. Godwin considers marriage to be "the most odious of all monopolies".
3. *The Scarlet Letter*, p. 185.
4. *Sadie*, after her conversion by a Protestant minister, sleeps with him which results in his self-slaughter and she joins again the old profession of harlotry.
5. In Antole France's novel, *Thais*, the actress-courtesan is converted to Christianity by a priest, but he himself is consumed by carnality.
6. *The Scarlet Letter*, p. 138.
7. Charles Boewe and Murray C. Murphy, from *American Literature*, XXXII, May, 1966, p. 202.
8. *The Scarlet Letter*, p. 5.
9. *Ibid.*, p. 118.
10. John Erskine, CHAL, II, pp. 26-27.
11. "Realm of Being and Dramatic Irony", in *From Hawthorne's Fiction: The Light and the Dark*, Norman: Uni. of Oklahoma Press, 1952.
12. Frederic I. Carpenter, "Scarlet A Minus", *College English*, V, Jan. 1994, p. 179.
13. *Ibid.*, p. 306.
14. *The Scarlet Letter*, p. 146.

15. *Ibid.*, p. 126.
16. David Tribe, "Our Free thought Heritage: The Humanist and Ethical Movement", *The Humanist Alternative: Some Definitions of Humanism*, ed. Paul Kurtz, London: Pembertone Books, 1973, p. 26.
17. *The Scarlet Letter*, p. 43.
18. *Ibid.*, p. 45.
19. *Ibid.*, p. 182.

Chapter 3

The Great Gatsby: A Critique of the American Dream of Success

The Great Gatsby (1925) is a profound commentary upon modern American as the descendant of a romantic frontier past in which idealism is as strong a component as materialism. Fitzgerald here questions the adequacy of modern America to sustain its heroic past. What he once said—"America's great promise is that something is going to happen but it never does. America is the moon that never rose"—can well serve as an epigraph for the novel which is a novel of ideas. A critic has rightly pointed out that *The Great Gatsby* "is not concerned with how people acquire money but how they use their wealth." Let us see who looks up for the moon to rise and whether it does rise.

Jay Gatsby, the protagonist, pursues this dream of romantic success without ever understanding that it has escaped him. The dream is to win Daisy back who once rejected him for his social position. Fitzgerald won Zelda with the power of writing, *This Side of Paradise* which established him as a voice of the Jazz-Age which is characterized by spend thrift, exuberance, wild parties, display of affluence and lack of morals and brought him at the age of 24, the wealth and fame he hungered after. Fitzgerald inherited from his mother's side a dream that any man in America could become anything through hardwork, honesty, determination and spiritual discipline but from his father's side he inherited a propensity for failure. This anti-thesis pervades his own life and most of his fiction. What Fitzgerald clearly felt that the dream pursued with less frantic, orgiastic, prideful convulsions of energy and spirit is the moral heart of the book. This he has shown by drawing Gatsby as a romantic hero and an epitome of the failure of the dream. The failure shows that he is a victim, not a hero, his death is pathetic, rather than tragic. His disappointments are the disappointments of all men whose idealistic dreams have been betrayed in the materialistic wasteland that America has become.

Malcolm Bradbury rightly observes that Gatsby embodies the symbolic aim of the book itself, a figure floating on the American dream symbolized by 'the green light'. The green light symbology is a central value in the novel. The novelist links it with Daisy who is for Gatsby the only promise of fulfillment that gleams beyond the green light that burns all night on her dock, the whole being of Gatsby exists in relation to what the green light symbolizes. In chapter V we have a fuller definition as to what it means in particular when Gatsby speaks to Daisy, standing at one of the windows of his mansion.

> "If it wasn't for the mist we could see your home across the bay," said Gatsby. "You always have a green light that burns all night at the end of your dock."
>
> Daisy put her arm through his abruptly, but he seemed absorbed in what he had just said. Possibly it had occurred to him that the colossal significance of that light had now vanished forever. Compared to the great distance that had separated him from Daisy it had seemed very near to her, almost touching her. It had seemed as close as a star to the moon. Now it was again a green light on a dock. His count of enchanted objects had diminished by one.[1]

Some say that this symbolism is vulgarized but it is not wholly true. If it is studied in its proper context, and the part it plays in conveying the message the book purports to convey, it is adequate to the problem it dramatizes. Marius Bewley rightly points out that the green light is successful because, part from its visual effectiveness, as it gleams across the bay, it embodies the profound naivete of Gatsby's sense of the future, while simultaneously suggesting the historicity of his hope. This note of historicity is not fully apparent at this point, of course. The symbol occurs several times, and most notably at the end.

> He had come a long way to this blue lawn, and his dream must have seemed so close that he could hardly fail to grasp it. He did not know that it was already behind him, somewhere back in that vast obscurity beyond the city, where the dark fields of the republic rolled on under the night.
>
> Gatsby believed in the green light, the orgiastic future that year by year recedes before us. It eluded us then, but that's no matter—tomorrow we will run faster, stretch out our arms farther.... And one fine morning....
>
> So we beat on, boats against the current, borne back ceaselessly into the past.[2]

The dream and the road, as taken by its pursuer, is symbolic. The dream stretches between a golden past and a golden future, but it is always frustrated by a desolate present—a moment of fruit rinds and discarded favours and crushed flowers.

As a Platonist, he is devoted to the pursuit of a 'vast, vulgar and meretricious beauty'. Gatsby, the son of the poor parents amasses great wealth by dubious means and changes his name from Jimmy Gatz to Jay Gatsby to outdistance his past. The choice of word 'Jay' is an imitation of the Jewishness to suggest richness which is material, not spiritual.

> His parents were shiftless and unsuccessful farm people—his imagination had never really accepted them as his parents at all. The truth was that Jay Gatsby of West Egg, Long Island, sprang from his Platonic conception of himself. He was a son of God—a phrase which, if it means anything, means just that—and he must be about his Father's business, the service of a vast, vulgar and meretricious beauty. So he invented just the sort of Jay Gatsby that a seventeen-year-old boy would be likely to invent, and to this conception he was faithful to the end.[3]

As a fabulously rich racketeer, much of his time is spent in trying to impress upon others the print of his wealth by throwing away lavish parties, even to those whom he does not know, nor do they know him. He dreams of transfiguring money into love which is an assault on reality, the system, the clock of time itself. "Society is decadent in one way, Gatsby in another."

His entry is dramatic in chapter III to explain the meaning of what Gatsby is. The novelist does not let us meet Gatsby face-to-face until he has concretely created this fantastic world of Gatsby's vision, for it is the element in which we must meet Gatsby if we are to understand his impersonal significance. The narrator tells,

> There was music from my neighbour's house through the summer nights. In his blue gadens men and girls came and went like moths among the whisperings and the champagne and the stars. At high tide in the afternoon I watched his guests diving from the tower of his raft, or taking the sun on the hot sand of his beach while his two motor-boats slit the waters of the Sound, drawing aquaplanes over cataracts of foam. On weekends his Rolls-Royce became an omnibus, bearing parties to and from the city between nine in the morning and long past midnight, while his station wagon scampered like a brisk yellow bug to meet all trains. And on Mondays eight servants, including an extra gardener, toiled all day with mops and scrubbing-brushes and hammers and garden-sheers, repairing the ravages of the night before.[4]

Gatsby's tragic flaw is that he is oblivious of the fact that the display of wealth without tradition is not sufficient for permanent entry into Daisy's world. When Gatsby intends to reveal their past relations, "I've got something to tell you, old sport,"[5] Daisy interrupts, "Please don't" and suggests that now they all should go home but Tom's curiosity is roused to know what that something could be.

> "I want to know what Mr Gatsby has to tell me."
>
> "Your wife doesn't love you," said Gatsby. "She's never loved you. She loves me."

> "You must be crazy!" Exclaimed Tom automatically.
>
> Gatsby sprang to his feet, vivid with excitement. "She never loved you, do you hear?" He cried. "She only married you because I was poor and she was tired of waiting for me. It was a terrible mistake, but in her heart she never loved anyone except me!"...
>
> "Sit down, Daisy," Tom's voice groped unsuccessfully for the paternal note. "What's been going on? I want to hear all about it."
>
> "I told you what's been going on," said Gatsby.
>
> "Going on for five years- and you didn't know."
>
> Tom turned to Daisy sharply.
>
> "You've been seeing this fellow for five years?"
>
> "Not seeing," said Gatsby. "No, we couldn't meet. But both of us loved each other all that time, old sport, and you didn't know. I used to laugh sometimes—but there was no laughter in his eyes—to think that you didn't know."
>
> "Oh—that's all." Tom tapped his thick fingers together like a clergyman and leaned back in his chair.
>
> "You're crazy!" he exploded. "I can't speak about what happened five years ago, because I didn't know Daisy then—and I'll be damned if I see how you got within a mile of her unless you brought the groceries to the back door. But all the rest of that's a God damned lie. Daisy loved me when she married me and she loves me now."
>
> "No," said Gatsby, "shaking his head."[6]

Despite her facile cynicism and claim to sophistication, Daisy is still the nice girl of Louisville town for Gatsby who, as he wants, denies ever loving Tom. He wants Daisy to say that he never loved Tom because in it he sees his prior claim of marriage to her in Louisville recognized. And Daisy speaks so to please Gatsby. "I never loved him", and turning to Gatsby says, "I love you now—isn't that enough? I can't help what's past." She began to sob helplessly. "I did love him once—but I loved you too."[7] Tom shatters Gatsby facade by openly accusing him of being a swindler, a bootlegger running that drug-stores business and to preserve his own gentleman's conception of womanly virtue and of the sanctity of his marriage.

The truth of Tom's accusation is too harsh to destroy Gatsby's dream of self-improvement which, he thinks, can be realized through partnership with Meyer Wolfsheim, but he does not know that "Wolfsheim is a case of misalliance as being the post-war successor to Dan Cody and to the ruthlessness and greed that once exploited a virgin West. He is the fabulous manipulator of bootleg gin rather than of copper, the modern man of legendary accomplishment "who fixed the World's Series back in 1919."

Nick Carraway is the narrator. His indictment of the materialist Buchanans is at the heart of the novel. Gatsby's defence and the denial of Tom's moral tirade fails to evoke the desired response in Daisy who "was drawing further and further into herself, so he gave that up and only the dead dream fought on as the afternoon slipped away trying to touch what was no longer tangible, struggling unhappily, undespairingly toward that lost voice across the room."[8]

It is Nick who brings Gatsby and Daisy together but still his dream of the 'golden-girl' remains elusive. When Daisy and Gatsby are driving back to Long Island from a party in New York, Daisy runs down Tom Buchanan's mistress, Myrtle Wilson in a 'hit-and-run' accident and does not stop. The yellow car belongs to Gatsby. Gatsby willingly takes the whole blame on him. He unintentionally tells Nick that it was Daisy at the wheel. Poisoned by Tom that Gatsby is responsible for Myrtle's death, because he is her lover which is a blatant lie and a vulgar demonstration of Iago-like 'motiveless villainy', Myrtle's husband, Wilson, goes to Gatsby's house and kills him in the swimming pool and then later kills himself too. Tom Buchanan, as virtually Gatsby's murderer by the crime he commits by proxy, is only a symbol of his deeper spiritual crime against Gatsby's inner vision. The funeral is attended by Nick and Gatsby's father, Henry C. Gatz, who thought that his son was a 'big man.' The irony is that none of his racketeers appears to attend the funeral. Even Daisy herself feels no remorse and "hadn't sent a message or a flower."[9]

> I tried to think about Gatsby then for a moment, but he was already too far away, and I could only remember, without resentment, that Daisy hadn't sent a message or a flower. Dimly I heard someone murmur 'Blessed are the dead that the rain falls on,' and then the owl-eyed man said 'Amen to that,' in a brave voice.
>
> We straggled down quickly through the rain to the cars. Owl-eyes spoke to me by the gate.
>
> "I couldn't get to the house," he remarked.
>
> "Neither could anybody else."
>
> "Go on!" He started. "Why, my God! They used to go there by the hundreds."
>
> He took off his glasses and wiped them again, outside and in. "The poor son-of-a-bitch", he said.[10]

This is a reflection of the shallowness of human relationship which was so prevalent in the 'twenties'.

However, we can say that the novel attacks the conventional values and opens rather than shuts the door to change. Nick's growing awareness of the Buchanan's destructiveness and Gatsby's blindness offers hope. His moral return to the safer and solid values of the heartland is a more substantial alternative to the "withering of the American dream" that the novel dramatizes.

Gatsby is destroyed by his illusions just as surely as the American landscape has been converted into a ghastly "valley of ashes." Gatsby seems to be encouraged by the very spirit of America of ambition and optimism but he does not know that the very spirit and idealism of the early settlers is destroyed by the materialistic concerns of the later settlers which is symbolized by the moving of all the Westerners—Gatsby, Daisy, Tom, Nick from a world of stable values into a moral vacuum. Gatsby's rejection of familial links and agrarian virtues, and his seduction to urban values destroyed the impulses of the dream. His corruption is related to historical corruption of the American spirit—the destruction of its early idealism by its involvement with a materialistic ethics.

Marius Bewley rightly points out that the great achievement of the novel is that it poetically evokes a sense of the goodness of that early dream, yet it offers at the same time the most damaging criticism of it in American literature:

> Gatsby, the "mythic" embodiment of the American dream, is shown in all his immature romanticism. His insecure grasp of social and human values, his lack of critical intelligence and self-knowledge, his blindness to the pitfalls that surround him in American society, his compulsive optimism, are realized in the text with rare assurance and understanding. And yet the very grounding of these deficiencies is Gatsby's goodness and faith in life, his compelling desire to realize all the possibilities of existence, his belief that we can have an Earthly Paradise populated by Buchanans. Fitzgerald has effectively suggested that these terrifying deficiencies are not so much the private deficiencies of Gatsby but are deficiencies inherent in contemporary manifestations of the American vision itself—"a vision no doubt" admirable, but stupidly defenceless before the equally American world of Tom and Daisy. Gatsby's deficiencies of intelligence and judgement bring him to his tragic death—a death that is spiritual as well as physical. But the more important question that faces us through our sense of the immediate tragedy is where they have brought America.[11]

What Fitzgerald wrote that "The whole burden of the novel is the loss of those illusions that give such colour to the world so that you don't care whether they are true or false, so long as they partake of the magical glory", finds support in T.S. Eliot that in Gatsby's pitiable disillusionment and defeat, Fitzgerald illustrates, the fever that burns away the spirited strength of so many Americans.

Notes

1. The parties, as hosted to impress Daisy with whom Gatsby had a brief affair before war, are the central value of the novel, "the epitome of the aristocratic rich and the sophisticated elite"

during the 20s. It is in these great gorgeous social gatherings that Nick understands the meaning of the word 'great', Fitzgerald tags with the hero in the title, the subject, being "an American morality, which is explored historically through the conflict between the surviving Puritan morality of the West and the post-war hedonism of the East," which is reflected, partly in the atmosphere pervading in the Jazz age tradition, as marked by lack of morals and class-consciousness: "the girls swooning, putting their heads on man's shoulders in a puppyish convivial way." Gatsby is the presiding genius of this comic revelry, verging on becoming great extravaganzas, yet what is interesting about it is that people with funny names who come to attend the parties know little about the host, nor does he know them personally.

2. F. Scott Fitzgerald, *The Great Gatsby*, New Delhi: Atlantic Publishers and Distributors, 1994, p. 105.
3. *Ibid*., p. 64.
4. *Ibid*., p. 65.
5. *Ibid*., p. 136.
6. *Ibid*., pp. 137-38.
7. *Ibid*., p. 139.
8. *Ibid*., p. 141.
9. *Ibid*., p. 72.
10. *Ibid*., pp. 181-82.
11. Marius Bewley, *The Sewanee Review*, Lxii (Spring, 1954).

Chapter 4

Concept of Freedom: Henry James' *The Portrait of a Lady*

In modern humanism, there is an emphasis on the twin principles of freedom and responsibility, responsibility is the curtailment of freedom, "the essence of moral life is bondage."[1] The humanist proposition that 'man is the measure of all things,' is misconstrued in the sense that 'measure of all things' does not mean that all is permissible. Man is free insofar as in his use of reason and intellect in regard to the discovery of truth. When we exercise choices, the key question which is to be kept in mind is whether the choices we make or the values we create are within human control and whether they are individualistic or promote collective good of mankind as a whole. Humanism does not hold that man is perfect or perfectable, and if there are 'no saints or utopias,' it does not mean that man should cease striving to rise to sainthood by being human. Humanism is attacked by its opponents for fostering evils, such as unbridled individualism, the lure of self-sufficiency to be a god unto himself which ironically drives man towards ruination. Since humanism as a philosophy is defined 'to render man more truly human' and 'make human life possible,' it be properly comprehended in the context of its founding principles and any departure, if sought from them, would jeopardize the very principle of human existence.

While examining Isabel Archer's view of freedom, which is one moral puzzle of the book, we have to keep in mind as to what precisely she, being a woman, means by freedom in a universe which is largely patriarchal. The twenty-three years grey-eyed young Isabel arrives at the Garden Court in London with her aunt, Mrs. Touchett, to, we are told, "see, to know, and to experience life." The quest is noble but there is every likelihood that, for want of illumination and moral vision, its purity may be destroyed. Isabel is introduced as an "interesting" and "independent" young lady. The two words are intriguing because in the 19th century, women were not free, as feminism had not made its passage into literature, the role, they were assigned by the patriarchs, was fixed, that they are for hearth, and thus the word 'independence' seems to have sinister associations, a tragic flaw, in Aristotelian sense. If it is economic independence, it is inadequate in that the concept of femininity is not characterized by economic freedom alone, if it is social, it might be taken as a departure from the accepted code of morality. The novelist throws no hint as to what it implies, he has left it open-ended. The tragic chord is struck when her candid expression about her view of self is totally misconceived. When to Ralph's question if his mother has adopted her, her reply that "she has not adopted me. I'm not a candidate for adoption. I'm very fond of my liberty"[2] shows that she is a complex character and her complex fate involves a complex dramatization which leaves much to reader's imagination.

Isabel has a great passion for knowledge, which has brought her to Europe to broaden her area of human understanding, she is described as "a young person of many theories, her imagination was remarkably active...as a prodigy of learning, a creature, reported to have read the classic authors in translations."[3] That Isabel's fanciful notion of freedom is complex and flawed becomes manifest in her encounters with people in the Old World, especially the prospective young men who come to propose her. The first is Lord Warburton, a specimen of English nobility for whom she has developed a liking but refuses to accept his marriage proposal saying "but I'm not sure I wish to marry anyone."[4] When he leaves the Garden Court, the residence of the Touchetts, in London, the novelist tells he "was evidently upset", but what he tells later about the young lady that she herself was upset is something curious and mystifying.

> What she felt was not a great responsibility, a great difficulty of choice; it appeared to her there had been no choice in the question. She couldn't marry Lord Warburton; the idea failed to support any enlightened prejudice in favour of the free exploration of life that she had hitherto entertained or was now capable of entertaining.[5]

The second to get Isabel's refusal is an American expatriate, Casper Goodwood, whose proposal has earlier been dismissed by her in Albany and who has written her a letter about his coming to meet her in England. The letter, she feels, has deprived her of "the sense of freedom", and it was this idea of diminished liberty to be so vital a factor, responsible for the rejection of "Lord Warburton's big bribe." Casper is the son of a rich cotton mill owner in Massachusetts, Isabel equally rejects Casper's proposal and to justify her view, she tells that she has also "refused a proposal of marriage last week—a dazzling one."[6]

> But I really don't want to marry, or to talk about it at all now. I shall probably never do it—no, never. I've a perfect right to feel that way, and it's no kindness to a woman to press her so hard, to urge her against her will.... It's not my fault; I can't marry you simply to please you. I won't say that I shall always remain your friend, because when women say that, in these situations, it passes, I believe, for a sort of mockery. But try me some day.[7]

What Isabel's last words "But try some day", means her indecisiveness or a prolonged snare to keep the prey's hopes alive? When Casper explains his position that "It's to make you independent that I want to marry you", Isabel's reply that "That's a beautiful sophism", is a product of a fertile wit and imagination but misprized, she continues to stress her idea of liberty.

> I'm not in my first youth—I can do what I choose—I belong quite to the independent class. I've neither father nor mother; I'm poor and of a serious disposition; I'm not pretty. I therefore am not bound to be timid and conventional; indeed I can't afford such luxuries.

> Besides, I try to judge things for myself; to judge wrong, I think, is more honourable than not to judge at all.[8]

Casper (or perhaps James) impresses upon her mind that it is in marriage that one is humanized, singleness in case of a woman is a social stigma and that "You'll get very sick of your independence," she curtly answers "Perhaps I shall; it's even very possible. When that day comes, I shall be glad to see you."[9] But the tone seems to be of defeatism and loss, which is reflected when, after Casper leaves the room, she, by an irresistible impulse, falls down on her knees, hiding her face in her arms, as if praying. The novelist comments,

> She was not praying; she was trembling—trembling all over. Vibration was easy to her, was in fact too constant with her, and she found herself now humming like a smitten harp. She only asked, however, to put on the cover, to case herself again in brown Holland, but she wished to resist her excitement, and the attitude of devotion, which she kept for some time, seemed to help her to be still.[10]

And when she rises, she feels that the 'tremor' had not subsided by then, the source of which was "the enjoyment she found in the exercise of her power", the power that gave her satisfaction was the refusal of the two ardent suitors in a fortnight, signifying her love of liberty. But what the novelist tells is something else and eventful. "The love of liberty of which she had given Caspar Goodwood so bold a sketch was as yet almost exclusively theoretic; she had not been able to indulge it on a large scale."[11]

When her friend, Henrietta Stackpole, a journalist, comes to know of her refusal to Casper, she puts, in right earnest, a question, "Do you know where you're drifting?" To it she says 'no', and likens her life metaphysically to a swift carriage in the blankness of the dark, which makes her idea of happiness ambivalent.

> "No, I haven't the least idea, and I find it very pleasant not to know. A swift carriage, of a dark night, rattling

with four horses over roads that one can't see—that's my idea of happiness."

"Mr. Goodwood certainly didn't teach you to say such things as that—like the heroine of an immoral novel," said Miss Stackpole. "You're drifting to some great mistake."

Isabel was irritated by her friend's interference, yet she still tried to think what truth this declaration could represent. She could think of no, thing that diverted her from saying: "You must be very fond of me, Henrietta, to be willing to be so aggressive."

"I love you intensely, Isabel," said Miss Stackpole with feeling.

"Well, if you love me intensely let me as intensely alone. I asked that of Mr. Goodwood, and I must also ask if you."

"Take care you're not let alone too much."

"That's what Mr. Goodwood said to me. I told him I must take the risks."

"You're a creature of risks—you make me shudder!" cried Henrietta. "When does Mr. Goodwood return to America?"

"I don't know—he didn't tell me."

"Perhaps you didn't enquire," said Henrietta "with the note of righteous irony."

"I gave him too little satisfaction to have the right to ask questions of him."

This assertion seemed to Miss Stackpole for a moment to bid defiance to comment; but at last she exclaimed: "Well, Isabel, if I didn't know you I might think you were heartless!"

"Take care," said Isabel; "you're spoiling me."[12]

The unease of the conversation of the two friends reveals that Isabel is blind to her romantic forays in the Old World where a handsome rich American girl is a prized 'catch' for fortune hunters. Tony Tanner has rightly pointed out that the source of her tragedy lies in the fact that in her ascent toward the world of ends, she is, in fact getting involved in the world of means. What Henrietta warns that "the perils for you is that you live too much in the world of your dreams", becomes a reality when her choice falls on a widower, Gilbert Osmond, a dabbler in art, who has a daughter, Pansy by a kept woman, Madam Merle. It is Madam Merle who steers Isabel into Osmond's orbit to evidently bring them together in marriage. Madam Merle is equally as Osmond is, a votary of selfish materialism, she has her eye on Isabel's rich dowry of seventy thousand pounds which is set aside by Ralph's generosity and wishful longings so as to make her see life as she intends to do. The plan badly unnerves his sister, the Countess Gemini who sees in it Isabel's predicament like that of 'a rabbit in the trap'. When Madam Merle says that "if he should marry Miss Archar, he'd behave like a gentleman,"[13] the Countess feels irritated and asks, "Do you mean as most gentleman behave?" which is a fine dig at Osmond's demonaic personality, he is a devil's disciple who wrecks destruction upon those around him, Madam, Merle, being one who cries out desperately "You've not only dried up my tears; you've dried up my soul"[14] at the end and after that her voice is not heard in the remaining pages. Osmond's imagination runs riot on knowing Isabel's fabulously rich fortune, and since he is projected as a class "collector" of beautiful things, he 'collects' Isabel, a beautiful specimen of nature and her money. The manner in which he patronizes a woman to win her confidence is calculating that it is hard to break its spell. To Isabel's question, "You're not conventional?," he says, "I like the way you utter that word! No, I'm not conventional, I'm convention myself. You don't understand that".[15] The irony is implicit, the word 'convention' has a 'catch', Isabel does not, and will never know what 'convention', he embodies.

The proposal of the two suitors, Warburton and Casper, is rejected for the reason that they seem to be "a collection of attributes", limited by their social positions and personal circumstances, and contrary to it, Osmond appears to her to be a pure personality, having no specific social position and material assets to define or to fix him. And thus by marrying Osmond, she feels, she will elude the fixedness of a definitive social role, she could be forcibly driven to play. But what she finds, instead, is her grinding "in the very mill of the conventional" to "collect" Isabel and her money like objects of art and thereby reduce her human identity to a 'portrait' in his art museum is one fine, illustration of Osmond's conventionality, which gives Isabel a sense of shock. Her entry into the world of Osmond, standing on "appearances" and "form" has been a case of error of judgement, a tragic flaw, where lies underneath her ambivalent notion of liberty. The truth is that Isabel is a victim of romantic liberation of self which comes on the fore in her discussion with Madam Merle in Chapter XIX.

Tony Tanner looks upon her marrying a widower nearly twice her age as "the result of a radical failure of vision, but the failure is not whimsical, it is rooted in her character." Her choice is governed by some obscure impulses. What aspect of Osmond's aestheticism has tainted her imagination, which hides underneath diabolism, is hard to guess, outside the fact that "she is fatally overwhelmed by the exterior glow of form and appearance of things."

Soon Isabel feels the heat of misalliance in marriage: she finds her husband being displeased by Ralph's visits to Rome where his mother, Mrs. Touchett, occupied a medieval palace, because Ralph, in Osmond's eyes was "an apostle of freedom", and he wished his wife to have no freedom of mind, fearing moral pollution. The thought of protest rises in her mind but she dismisses thinking that it would amount to break up with Osmond and a break with him once would be a break for ever. Besides the puritan heritage; "all the traditionary decencies and sanctities of marriage", are strong in her mind to keep the piety of the sacrament protected.

Notwithstanding, what goes off between her and Henrietta is a reflection of a dismal story of failed dreams and hopes, which is a direct offshoot of her flawed concept of liberty and independence. Henrietta asks her as to why she looks so wretched and miserable, Isabel makes a confession of what has begun to plague her.

> "Yes, I'm wretched," she said very mildly. She hated to hear herself say it; she tried to say it as judicially as possible.
>
> "What does he do to you?" Henrietta asked, frowning as if she were enquiring into the operations of a quack doctor.
>
> "He does nothing. But he doesn't like me."
>
> "He's very hard to please!" cried Miss Stackpole. "Why don't you leave him?"
>
> "I can't change that way," Isabel said.
>
> "Why not, I should like to know? You won't confess that you've made a mistaken. You're too proud."
>
> "I don't know whether I'm too proud. But I can't publish my mistake. I don't think that's decent. I'd much rather die."
>
> "You won't think so always," said Henrietta.
>
> "I don't know what great unhappiness might bring me to" but it seems to me "I shall always be ashamed. One must accept one's deeds. I married him before all the world; I was perfectly free; it was impossible to do anything more deliberate. One can't change that way," Isabel repeated.
>
> "You have changed, in spite of the impossibility. I hope you don't mean to say you like him."
>
> Isabel debated. "No, I don't like him. I can tell you, because I'm weary of my secret. But that's enough; I can't announce it on the housetops."
>
> Henrietta gave a laugh. "Don't you think you're rather too considerate?"
>
> "It's not of him that I'm considerate—it's of myself!" Isabel answered.[16]

Since Pansy is Madam Merle's daughter by Osmond, the two want that she be married to Lord Warburton, and for it they intend to exploit Isabel's relation with him, which is a cardinal sin in Jamesian world of fiction. Isabel is kept in the dark about this conspiracy, the matter grows all she more complex when Lord Warburton's visitations to Rome are mistaken by Osmond and Madam Merle that he comes because he has taken a fancy on Pansy, whereas the reality, as we know, is altogether different. Why they press so hard upon Isabel to persuade Lord Warburton to marry Pansy is plain which is to "collect" Warburton's fortune as he did Isabel's. Her dilemma of morality and value clashes with Osmond's philosophy of "appearances" which is a variant of supposed sophistication. Osmond is unaware of the nature of sin which is the sin of incest; the lovers are the lovers of both mother and daughter. When Madam Merle comes back from Naples, she finds the ruins of the tragic failure of her plan, and at once concludes that perhaps it could be Isabel's doing for the fact that she has marked the English Lord for her own self, thereby ruining Pansy's future, which is another case of blatant misconception.

> If Lord Warburton simply got tired of the poor child, that's one thing and it's a pity. If he gave her up to please you it's another. That's a pity too, but in a different way.[17]

Isabel is terribly shaken by such acts of insolence and monstrously false accusations which have aggravated her disappointments. She wonders if this is what Osmond means by 'convention', she feels that Osmond has betrayed her in words and thoughts, and the knowledge of it is like "a drop of corrosive acid upon an open wound." She is confronted with a conviction that Osmond has married her like a vulgar adventurer for money, which is the worst that could have happened to her and which has happened; she foresees something more worse to happen. She reconciles with Osmond's 'collecting' her money but she wants him to accept the truth of it and tell her that he married her for money. A question rises in her mind—"Would he take her money and let her go?"[18]

By degrees Isabel becomes aware of her own folly and miscalculations. The illusion shatters. She finds hard to breathe in the stuffy and cramped atmosphere in Osmond's villa. In Madam Merle's saddest cry, "Have I been so vile for nothing?"[19], she sees her own tragedy. The freedom that she has attained in Osmond's house is a travesty of her earlier idea of freedom with which she came to Europe. The place becomes a 'hot land', symbolic of spiritual tormentation and unimaginable physical sufferings. In the existing situation, she looks for an 'exit' but it is too late.

Nevertheless, the 'exit' comes when she comes to Garden Court to see Ralph dying and meets Casper there, much against her expectations. She is caught in a dilemma whether to go back to Osmond or begin a fresh living elsewhere. She hears nothing from Pansy even, to whom she promised to return, perhaps her father had asked her not to write. In Goodwood's kiss, she sees "a very straight path"[20] to no other place but Rome. Isabel's return to Rome has become much debatable. Some ask, when she has come to 'see' and 'experience' life, what life she had seen by her association with a bourgeois who is all phoney and fake? Those who say that she should have stayed back in London and married a suitor of her choice forget that she is a married woman, and is bound by the piety of the sacrament. For a married woman, a husband's home is the legitimate dwelling to inhabit. The puritanical heritage has mellowed down in her and therefore her choice to fly into Rome is moral and shows that she has attained the most vital aspect of liberty, which is freedom from illusions. James himself was conscious of a possible criticism. In his Note books, he observes:

> The obvious criticism of course will be that it is not finished—that I have not seen the heroine to the end of her situation—that I have left her en l'air. This is both true and false. The whole of anything is never told; you can only take what groups together.... It is complete in itself.

The 'return to Rome' has freed the Being from the twisted vision and confused values. Now Isabel would live life on her own terms and would never fall a victim of deceptions and calculations of a worldling like Osmond. She has seen the curves of life from close quarters and has evolved her own vision to live by.

Notes

1. John Herman Randall Jr, "What is the Temper of Humanism", Paul Kurtz (ed.) *The Humanist Alternative: Some Definitions of Humanism*, London: Pemberton Books, 1973, p. 59.

2. Henry James, *The Portrait of a Lady*, Delhi: Oxford University Press, 1981, p. 18.
3. *Ibid.*, p. 51.
4. *Ibid.*, p. 114.
5. *Ibid.*, p. 117.
6. *Ibid.*, p. 169.
7. *Ibid.*, p. 167.
8. *Ibid.*, p. 172.
9. *Ibid.*, p. 173.
10. *Ibid.*, p. 175.
11. *Idem.*
12. *Ibid.*, pp. 177-78.
13. *Ibid.*, p. 293.
14. *Ibid.*, p. 569.
15. *Ibid.*, p. 337.
16. *Ibid.*, pp. 531-32.
17. *Ibid.*, p. 567.
18. *Ibid.*, p. 566.
19. *Ibid.*, p. 572.
20. *Ibid.*, p. 644.

Chapter 5

Existential Concerns in Eugene O'Neill's *The Hairy Ape*

The Hairy Ape is a play about the problem of existence, as confronted by modern man in a highly mechanized post-war American society. The existential concerns are reflected in the protagonist's failure to comprehend the nature of reality and in his attempt to coming to terms with it by cherishing his own illusions which ironically drive him to death, which is the only solution, perhaps the play dramatizes. In the post-war period, all political institutions/philosophies evolved to ameliorate the crucial conditions of living and the illusion, as generated by the murmur of the radical movement, shattered, the psychoanalysts. Freud and Jung—found the inside story of the various unconscious mechanism which were interpreted responsible for human behaviour, not encouraging: if the external world is cruel, the internal world of psyche is also dark and diabolic, the reality being incapable to unearth. During the years 1921-22, O'Neill wrote plays on the themes, such as the evils of economic differentiation, industrialism, class antagonism, individualism, social justice and democracy but above all what arrested his attention was the problem of alienation and man's disorientation and bewilderment from within and from without.

It is a play about the stokehole life which evokes the vision of hell. Yank is at the centre of action, it is his play. The two other characters are Long, a radical and Paddy, who sees an escape from the horrors of the mechanistic materialism in going back to the past.

> Oh! to be back in the fine days of my youth, Ochone! Oh, there was fine beautiful ships them days—clippers wid tall masts touching the sky—fine strong men in them—men that was sons of the sea if't as the mother that bore them. Oh, the clean skin of them, and the clear eyes, the straight backs and full chest of them! Brave men they was, and bold men surely! We'd be sailing out, bound down round the Horn maybe. We'd be making sail in the dawn with a fair breeze, singing a chanty song wid no care to it. And astern the land would be sinking low and dying out, but we'd give it not heed but a laugh, and never a look behind. For the day that was, was enough, for we was free men—and I'm thinking 'tis only slaves doer giving heed to the day that's gone or the day to come—until they're old like me.[1]

But can this sort of sentimentalism make man to surmount the problem of existence?

The existentialists, both theistic and atheistic, show concern with the problem of suicide. In the Preface to *The Myth of Sisyphus*, Camus says that the fundamental subject is whether life has a meaning. Herbert Read in the Foreword to *The Rebel* writes that the book has a logic which is the logic of the justifiability of the act of rebellion which is existential in nature and conception: man is confronted with a choice what is to be endured/or not endured in face of the terror of history and the crucial conditions of living to keep his humanity and freedom protected. Just as "*The Myth* begins with a meditation on living or not living—on the implication of the act of suicide, *The Rebel* begins with a meditation on enduring or not enduring on the implication of the act of rebellion."[2] It is this problem of suicide that haunted O'Neill's mind and the genesis of *The Hairy Ape* owes to it which he explained to an interviewer for the American magazine in 1922.

> I shouldn't have known the stokers if I hadn't happened to scrape an acquaintance with one of our own furnace

> room gang at Jimmy the Priest's. His name was Driscoll, and he was a Liverpool Irishman...the synonym for the tough customer...Driscoll...came to a strange end. He committed suicide by jumping overboard in mid-ocean.... Why? It was the why of Driscoll's suicide that gave me the germ of the idea....[3]

Continuing the idea as expressed in the above statement, O'Neill explains how Driscoll's suicide grew into the play.

> The search for an explanation of why Driscoll, proud of his animal superiority and incomplete harmony with his limited conception of the universe, should kill himself provided the germ idea for *The Hairy Ape*.[4]

And thus the play turns out to be a fine attempt to "probe in the shadow of the soul of man, bewildered by the disharmony of his primitive pride and individualism at war with the mechanistic development of the society."

Sartre makes a distinction between unconscious being (Being-in-itself) and conscious being (Being-for-itself) on the basis of their priority of structure, self knowledge and the limits of the potentialities and possibilities. The Being-in-itself is not a subject of change, it is self-contained what it is, while Being-for-itself is a subject of change, it is always in state of transcendence and has the capacity to evolve. For Sartre, man is Being-for-itself, a 'project', which he identifies with freedom, consciousness and transcendence. "Consciousness is consciousness of something. This means that transcendence is the constitutive structure of consciousness: that is that consciousness is born, supported by a being which is not itself."[5] Husserl too defines consciousness as a transcendence by means of which a meaning of being beyond being is revealed.

The Being-in-itself is and exists. It can never be other than what it is. It is as full as an egg.

> It is full positivity. It knows no otherness, it never posits itself as other than another being. It can support no connection with the other. It is itself indefinitely and it exhausts itself in being.[6]

Contrary to it, the Being-for-itself is in the continuous process of negating itself to be what it is not and is not what it is. It is in act of nihilating that it becomes capable of evolving itself to fill the lack or the void and therefore it is always in the state of flight from itself, Sartre calls it 'bad faith' and says that this can be understood by postulating consciousness that is within itself separated from itself. By negating cowardice, the notion of courage rises which shows that the two consciousness remain in one self at the same time and it is in this sense that Sartre postulates the concept of being for itself as something that it is not what it is. He gives the example of a soldier, a tailor, a grocer to explicate his viewpoint: a man is not a soldier or a grocer in the sense a table is a table and a glass is a glass.

This concept of Being's ontology becomes manifest in Yank's progression/regression of consciousness which comes into the world by man. The scene opens on a trans-Atlantic liner. A world of stokers is introduced who by their dialect and dress are removed from the human world and thus look primitive. Yank is seen sitting in the front, broader, fiercer and more truculent than others, he is respected for his physical superiority and confidence in himself. The stokers eat, drink and sing which makes the place look bohemian. We hear voices of the stokers, they are not given any name or identity which is the predicament of the working class that man in capitalism is reduced to an automaton.

> Ha, ha, ha,
> Drink, do not think!
> Drink, do not think!
> Drink, do not think![7]

From the start the problem of the existence and the worker's exploitation in a class society is hinted at in Long's estimate of the capitalist class who are "Lazy bloated swine" in his eyes and who use religion as a facade. Long is a radical, and progressive-minded person who believes in the freedom and equality of all. He feels excited to hear Yank call the ship a hell.

> Listen 'ere, Comrades! Yank 'ere is right. 'E says this 'ere stinkin' ship is our 'ome. And e says as 'ome is 'ell. And 'e's right! This is 'ell. We live in 'ell, Comrades—

> and right enough we'll die in it.... But what d' they care for the Bible—them lazy, bloated swine what travels first cabin? Them's the ones. They dragged us down til we're on'y wage slaves in the bowels of a bloody ship, sweatin', burnin' up, eatin' coal-dust! Hit's them's ter blame—the damned capitalist class.[8]

But Yank does not agree with Long that the life in the stokehole is hellish which is a reflection of his consciousness of physical strength and which he considers commensurate with a stoker's job, he calls it 'A man's job' for which he is ridiculed by voices.

John Macquarrie writes, "for all the existentialists the subject is the 'existent' in the whole range of his existing. He is not only a 'thinking subject' but an initiator of action and a centre of feeling. It is this whole spectrum of existence, known directly and concretely in the very act of existing, that existentialism tries to express."[9] In the traditional Western philosophy since the time of Descartes the 'self as subject' has been a subject of study in existentialism and by 'subject' they mean the "thinking subject", In John Macmurray[10] "self as agent" is a central theme.

What is Yank as "thinking subject"? What he thinks about is a reflection of his own illusions of life of a stokehole, which evaporates into nothingness like smoke in Scene Three. Glancing at Long, he says,

> Wanter know what I think? Yuh ain't no good for no one. Yuh're de bunk. Yuh ain't got no noive, get me? Yuh're yellow, dat's what. Yellow, dat's you. Say! What's dem slobs in de foist cabin got to do wit us? We're better men dan dey are, ain't we? Sure! One of us guys could clean up de whole mob wit one mit. Put one of 'em down here for one watch in de stokehole, what'd happen? Dey'd carry him off on a stretcher. Dem boids don't amount to nothin'. Dey're just baggage. Who makes dis old tub run? Ain't it us guys? Well den, we belong don't we? We belong and dey don't. Dat's all.[11]

Yank is not wholly wrong in his analysis of the bourgeois hegemony of the ruling class and the role that it plays in creating the crucial conditions of living. But Yank's sense of belongingness to the stokehole life, differing from that of the other stokers, is a point of interest and the very strength of the play. He calls Paddy old "Yuh're too old" and himself young, "I'm young! I'm in de pink!", being unaware of ironic implication that this act of self-glorification is tragic and ephemeral. He says Paddy cannot breathe and swallow cold dust but he can.

> I kin, see? Dat's fresh air for me! Dat's food for me! I'm new, get me? Hell in de stokehole? Sure! It takes a man to work in hell. Hell, sure, dat's my fav'rite climate. I eat it up! I git fat on it! It's me makes it hot! It's me makes it roar! It's me makes it move! Sure, on'y for me everyting stops.[12]

The illusion of the physical superiority and self-glorification shatters in Scene Three in an encounter which is constructed on the widening existing gap between the two classes, the have and have-nots. Mildred Douglas, the daughter of the steel tycoon, is introduced who runs the liner. She is a student of sociology and her interest, we are told, is to see how the other half lives which is a gesture of sympathy, we appreciate. She is taken into the stokehole which throws the lurid shades of hell, wherein the stokers are cramped like entrapped apes, resembling the Neanderthal Man in the pictures. The encounter is made dramatic by projecting Yank in a fiercely grotesque posture, angering at the engineer's whistle which he takes as an assault on his pride.

> Come down and I'll moider yuh! Pullin' dat whistle on me, huh? I'll show yuh! I'll crach yer skull in! I'll drive yer teet' down yer troat! I'll slam yer nose trou de back of yer head! I'll cut yer guts out for a nickel, yuh lousey boob, yuh dirty, crummy, muck eatin' son of a—.[13]

The sight of a hairy-chested man, naked upto the waist, has a shattering impact on Mildred's sensibility. She is on verge of fainting, she only could speak, "Take me away! Oh, the filthy beast."[14] The remark is directed, not against Yank but against the system and its soulless philosophy of mechanization of society which is not different from the ironic mechanization of man and, by implication, suggests change in the working conditions so as to make him escape the tragic conversion into a beast. But it is sad that Yank takes it as an expression of bourgeois class pride and superiority and resents it in rather an impulsive manner, which is seen in his running after the engineers who take Mildred out, brandishing a shovel which falls with a clang on the steel gate. The encounter is momentary but it is eventful in the sense that its impact is total. Yank's existential self is wrenched away from its existential roots. He comes out of the world of the stokers in state of utter bewilderment into the world of men in search of Mildred whom he does not meet till he is crushed to death by a gorilla, symbolizing his own primitive past. Yank's watch has just come off, the other stokers have washed their faces and body but Yank stands as a contrast to them "a blackened brooding figure", sitting on a bench in the exact attitude of Rodin's 'The Thinker' which is a sure sign of loss of self and uprootedness. Long takes Mildred's visit as a mortifying gesture, an assault on the proletariat.

> Hinsultin' us! Hinsultin us, the bloody cow! And them bloody engineers! What right 'as they got to be exhibitin' us 's if we was bleedin' monkeys in a menagerie? Did we sign for hinsults to our dignity as 'onest workers? Is that in the ship's articles? You kin bloody well bet it ain't! But I knows why they done it.[15]

Paddy interprets Yank's indifference to self as a case of love at first sight, sarcastically "Sure it was as if she'd seen a great hairy ape escaped from the zoo."[16] Yank accepts reality as to what a worker can be in capitalism other than a beast. He becomes conscious of his being called 'a hairy ape' and from here onward he sees himself as what Mildred called him which is a reflection of the primitive unconsciousness. He is human, not a beast. Rising frenziedly from the bottom of the heap, he brushes aside the rest stokers and moves out to show Mildred "Who's a ape."

> Hairy ape, huh? Sure! Dat's de way she looked at me, aw right. Hairy ape! So dat's me, huh? [Bursting into rage—as if she were still in front of him] Yuh skinny tart! Yuh white-faced slut, yuh! I'll show yuh who's a ape![17]

Long and Yank come to the Fifth Avenue, a locality of the rich, in search of Mildred and what happens to them there is a powerful reflection of the attitude of the rich to the poor which is a bane of social inequality and economic differentiation. Mildred becomes Yank's obsession, he is seized over by a fury of revenge "Christ I'll fix her."[18] Long explains to Yank that it is not a personal matter between him and Mildred, but a clash of the two classes, the rich and the poor,

> Ain't that why I brought yer up 'ere—to show yer? Yer been lookin' at this 'ere 'ole affair wrong. Yer been actin' an' talkin's if it was all a bleedin' personal matter between yer and that bloody cow. I wants to convince yer she was on'y a representative of 'er clarss. I wants to awaken yer bloody clarss consciousness. Then yer'll see it's 'er clarss yer've got to fight, not 'er alone. There's a 'ole mob of 'em like 'er, Gawd blind 'em![19]

Long impresses upon Yank the futility of the use of force in the modern age of industry wherein the economy is the strength, the power to rule which is why the Marxist revolutionary overthrow of the bourgeois hegemony proved to be a weak weapon. It is Sunday, the crowd is coming out after the Church service. Men are moving carelessly, talking about American Bazar, income tax, false principles and the radicals. No one seems to be interested in the two. But Yank to assert his force makes an effort to pull out a pole and bumps into a gentle man who is running for a bus. He cries for help, the officers appear and Yank is arrested and is confined in a jail where the steel bars generate illusion that it is his creation and Yank continues to be brutal in a bid to bend the bars to sustain the illusion that he is still undefeated.

The problem of existence as confronted by him remains ironically unresolved in the office of the I.W.W. which is an organization, working to protect the interest of the proletariat class. In the prison Yank hears the name of I.W.W. the reality of which is read out by the impersonal voices.

> I refer to that devil's brew of rascals, jail-birds, murderers, and cut-throats who libel all honest working men by calling themselves the Industrial Workers of the World; but in the light of their nefarious plots, I call them the Industrious Wreckers of the World![20]

Notwithstanding, the word 'wreckers' fires Yank's imagination. "Wreckers, dat's de right dope! Dat belongs! Me before dem!" which suggests senselessness of violence and destruction that takes man nowhere. And surprisingly enough when Yank talks of dynamite, he is suspected to be a spy of some business tycoon.

SECRETARY	[with pretended carelessness] You mean, change the unequal conditions of society by legitimate direct action—or with dynamite?
YANK	Dynamite! Blow it offen de oith—steel—all de cages—all de factories, steamers, buildings, jails—de Steel Trust and all dat makes it go.[21]

And therefore for his failure to understand the implication of the I.W.W. which believes in legitimate action, Yank is thrown out as "a brainless ape" on the pavement where his encounter with a policeman further aggravates the dilemma of existence. To his question, "Say, where do I go from here?" the policeman's reply "Go to hell"[22] is no viable answer to solve the problem of the workers in a class society.

And ultimately the search for Mildred takes him to a monkey house at a zoo where his encounter with a gorilla, his own past, is equally disasterous. The entry of the human is a sort of trespassing in the world of animals which is suggested by the angry chatterings and screechings of the animals but Yank's unconscious primitive self takes it a welcoming gesture and at once establishes his belongingness. He fails to fully comprehend its reality. The scene is a long monologue. Yank's dialogue with the gorilla is an attempt to come to terms with the reality of the past because the present has rejected him but this too turns out to be fatal.

> So yuh're what she seen when she looked at me, de white-faced tart! I was you to her, get me? On'y outa de cage—broke out—free to moider her, see? Sure! Dat's what she tought. She wasn't wise dat I was in a cage, too—worser'n yours—sure—a damn sight—'cause you

got some chanct to bust loose—but me—[he grows confused] Aw, hell! It's all wrong, ain't it?[23]

Yank thinks of taking the gorilla to the Fifth Avenue for a walk and show to the world that he has got a real companion which shows that the thinking faculty in Yank, which is denied to the animals, is destroyed for want of its proper application to finding out the means to resolve the problem of existence. His idea of fighting man's enemy to man by taking animals as companion is a quixotic feat of idiotic imaginings which drive man to death. Man has to fight his own battle as man, it is folly to look toward any outer agency outside the human. This is what means by gorilla's murderous hug. Yank is crushed to death, he painfully mutters, "Even him didn't tink I belonged." And then what with sudden despair, he cries out, "Christ where do I get off at? Where do I fit in?"[24]

O'Nell himself explained the tragic dilemma of Yank in 1924 that "Yank can't go forward, so he tries to go back. This is what his shaking hands with the gorilla meant. But he can't go back to belong either. The gorilla kills him." The struggle in the past used to be between man and destiny, today it is between man and his environment, between man and his own self. If man conforms to the values of the modern world, he, being misfit, dies a spiritual death, and if he does not, he is rejected by it. This is the dilemma of existence. And therefore what man should do, as the existentialist would have it, is to evolve his own values and live by them.

Notes

1. *The Hairy Ape*, Penguin Books Ltd., 1960, p. 143.
2. Herbert Read, Foreword to *The Rebel*, Penguin Books Ltd., 1975, p. 7.
3. Quoted in R.S. Singh, *O'Neill The Playwright*, Delhi: Doaba House, 1971, p. 106.
4. *Idem.*
5. "The Pursuit of Being", in *Being and Nothingness*, New York: Gramercy Books, 1956, p. LXI.
6. *Ibid.*, p. LXVI.
7. *The Hairy Ape*, p. 140.

8. *Ibid.*, p. 141.
9. John Macquarrie, *Existentialism*, Penguin Books Ltd., 1975, pp. 14-15.
10. John Macmurray, *The Self as Agent*, New York, London, 1957, p. 84.
11. *The Hairy Ape*, p. 142.
12. *Ibid.*, pp. 145-46.
13. *Ibid.*, pp. 156-57.
14. *Ibid.*, p. 157.
15. *Ibid.*, p. 159.
16. *Ibid.*, p. 162.
17. *Idem.*
18. *Ibid.*, p. 163.
19. *Ibid.*, p. 167.
20. *Ibid.*, p. 175.
21. *Ibid.*, pp. 182-83.
22. *Ibid.*, p. 183.
23. *Ibid.*, pp. 186-87.
24. *Ibid.*, p. 189.

Chapter 6

Ontology in William Faulkner's *The Sound and the Fury*

Ontology is put forth as "the science or philosophy of being" it is "that branch of metaphysics which examines the existence, or essence of things, producing a theory about what exists or a list of things that exist."[1] Hazel Barnes defines ontology as the study "of the structures of being of the existent taken as totality."[2]

Sartre in *Being and Nothingness*, as the title indicates, which is a study of the human condition, shows that "man is the being by whom Nothingness comes into the world, this means that man is himself Being and Nothingness." In other words, the being is always in the process of becoming what it is not by means of Nothingness, which fashions the original choice of Being by which "the real individuals have made themselves what they are". The consciousness is one variant of Nothingness, which is the consciousness of being 'Other' which is also a fundamental category, i.e. Being-with-others in regard to human relationship. This is what we call the "ontological proof."[3]

Sartre discusses the two radically distinct dimensions of Being-in-itself (unconscious) and Being-for-itself (conscious) which is what is has to be because it is what it is not. But because the Fort-itself is dependent on In-itself both in its origin and in its continued history, it includes the Being-in-itself which is what it is, complete in itself as an egg is an egg and no other than the egg or a table is a table, no other than a table. This division of the

Being into two-In-itself and For-itself is applied to all categories of the existents. "The For-itself is like a tiny nihilation which has its origin at the heart of Being; and this nihilation is sufficient to cause a total upheaval to happen to In-itself. This upheaval is the world."[4]

The Being-in-itself is what it simply exists, it is totally incapable of being other than what it is. It is self-contained, having no trace of duality, it is fullness as full as a egg.

> The in-itself is full of itself, and no more plentitude can be imagined, no more perfect equivalence of content to container. There is not the slightest emphasis in being not the tinier crack through which nothingness might slip in.[5]

Opposed to it, the For-itself is what it is not and is not what it is, and thus in order to be fully what it is, it is in a continuous process of negating itself. It is capable of change or evolution and by questioning its own being, transcends its own being. Therefore, it is always in the state of flight from itself which Sartre terms as "bad faith", which is to expose the duality of the deceived and the deceiver.[6]

A question arises whether ontology can formulate any ethical precepts, and if there are any, how they are related to the creation of value which alone makes the process of evolution a possibility? The answer to it is simple that ontology does formulate the ethico-moral principles of existence the realisation of which takes place, while confronting human reality in a given situation. Ontology thus, as the science of being, reveals to us the origin and nature of value "in relation to which the for-itself determines its being as a lack." And it is the lack or the void which haunts the For-itself to be fully what it wants to be because for want of it, it loses its very authenticity.

A look into the mould, the characters are cast into, shows how the ontological premises become manifest in the novel. The two worlds figure in *The Sound and the Fury*: the first is the white world of the Compsons which is deeply related with the novelist's own estimate that "it is the story of blood gone bad," and the second is of the blacks, the strength of

which lies in the objectification of the niceties and warmth of human love, transcending the subjectivity and barriers of racial discrimination. The characters are divided into two distinct categories, representing the two modes of Being-the first includes those who are in the state of In-itself which is a state of moral inertness and passivity, born of a lack of will and vision to be what it is not; the second includes those who are projected as the very exemplification of the For-itself mode of existence and are invested with a worldview and capacity to evolve themselves into a mode of existence, they feel, it is denied. To fully appreciate the thesis of the novel which dramatizes the doom and disintegration of a single Southern aristocratic family of Jafferson town in Mississippi we have to keep in mind what Robert Penn Warren says that "the scene of the enactment of the doom, for all practical purposes, takes places within the four walls of the Compson house, and the doom is enacted inside the heads of the people who live within those four walls." It is a sad comment on the failure of the Compson in their attempt to break those imprisoning barriers of self to be other than what they have become by inherited doom that has befallen the family. But it is also a reflection of their irresponsible bohemianistic proclivities and unbridled individualism, verging on vulgar hedonistic acquisitiveness and selfish materialism. The critic perhaps has also in mind the negativistic traits the Compson children inherit, consciously or unconsciously, for one or the other reason, being unaware of the tragic ironies whether the life, they are likely to be drifted toward, has a meaning or it is all, "full of sound and fury/ Signifying nothing".

It is learnt that there is a curse on the family, but of what precise nature it is, is not specified, and whether the curse has doomed the father and the mother alone, or they have doomed, by their collaboration, the Compson children too, thereby making it "an inherited doom", which is an interesting study in the ontology of the Being. If thy fail to live upto the old image, at least what they can do is not to demean themselves to a level so as to lose their human identity.

What of the Compsons parents—Richmond Compson and Caroline Compson? Jason Richmond Compson III is a descendant

of an illustrious aristocratic Southern family, with a lineage of governor and brigadier-general, now on decline. He is the son of a general, but finding himself untenable to live upto their moral idealism, takes to drinking, thinking "that liquor teaches you to confuse the means with the ends", signifying confusion of values which distorts vision. Instead of doing something positive to overcome the crisis, he develops an utter pessimistic philosophy of life which makes things all the more blighted. He looks upon every human act and experience absurd and meaningless, being unaware of the fact that such an anti-human philosophy would cast a morally ruinous impact upon the sensibility of the children.

Richmond is a lawyer, it is told, but, strangely enough, we are not told anything about his professional acumen, instead, his views on time, misfortunes, war, women and virginity are so revolting that one could hardly believe. One such vital fragmentary utterance is about time. Giving a clock to Quentin, he says, "Quentin, I give you the mausoleum of all hope and despair".... Because no battle is ever won he said. They are not even fought. The field only reveals to man his own folly and despair, and victory is an illusion of philosopher and fools."[7] Quentin takes a clock because "father said clocks slay time. He said time is dead as long as it is being clicked off by little wheels; only when the clock stops does time come to life."[8] When the father is told about Caddy's pregnancy, he shows disinterestedness and says,

> In the South, you are ashamed of being a virgin. Boys. Men. They lie about it. Because it means less to women, Father said. He said it was men invented virginity, not women.[9]

Quentin recalls in passage wondering how his father disaffiliated himself from all social ties like a beatnik which is reflected when Caddy's freedom grows alarming and there is a need to put her activities under surveillance.

> I won't have my daughter spied on I wouldn't have.
>
> How can I control any of them when you have always taught them to have no respect for me and my wishes I know you look down on my people but is that any

> reason for teaching my children my own children I suffered for to have no respect.
>
> I will not have my daughter spied on by you or Quentin or anybody no matter what you think she has done.
>
> At least you agree there is reason for having her watched.
>
> I wouldn't have I wouldn't have. I know you wouldn't I didn't mean to speak so sharply but women have no respect for each other for themselves.[10]

Caroline Compson is also projected as a totally negative character. A critic has held her wholly responsible for the break up of the Compson family. She is delineated as a highly cold, self-centred neurotic mother who is more alive to the social position of her family (the Basecombs) rather than showing concern with her own family. Faulkner, Quentin recalls, has painted her as a self-pitying, invalid, egocentric, petulant and whining.

> Mother lay back in her chair, the camphor handkerchief to her mouth. Father hadn't moved he still sat beside her holding her hand the bellowing hammering away like no place for it in silence.[11]

She is a mother, devoid of any motherly instinct which is reflected in Quentin's yearnings for motherly love in his monologue, "If I'd just had a mother so I could say Mother Mother."[12] She is complaining all the time against her husband, children and the cruelties of fate.

> Benjamin was punishment enough for any sins I have committed I thought he was my punishment for putting aside my pride and marrying a man who held himself above me.[13]

How much she feels concerned about Caddy's well-being, and how she disowns the birth of children but Jason which is a blatant shame on the institution of motherhood, comes on the fore beautifully by a technique of self-mockery.

> ...she is no better than that when I was a girl I was unfortunate I was only a Bascomb I was taught that there is no half-way ground that a woman is either a lady or not but I never dreamed when I held her in my

> arms that any daughter of mine could let herself.... Let me have Jason and you keep the others they are not my flesh and blood like he is strangers nothing of mine and I am afraid of them I can take Jason and go where we are not known I'll go down on my knees and pray for the absolution of my sins that he may escape this curse to try to forget that the others ever were.[14]

She burns Caddy's cheques saying "We Basecombs need no body's charity. Certainly not of a 'fallen' woman."[15] One can ask, if taking the birth of a congenital child a punishment, which is all a freak of biological determinism, and burning the currency notes is characteristic of the Basecomb pride she often speaks high of it, then the question whether the doom is acquired or inherited becomes virtually an interesting study for the anthropologists and the psychoanalysts to explore its genesis and leaves nothing skeptical about the fact that in the hands of such creatures' life certainly tends to be

> ...a tale
> Told by an idiot, full of sound and fury
> Signifying nothing[16]

The truth is that both Richmond and Caroline are a live extension of the Being-in-itself mode of existence, not only in 'representation' but in acts and thoughts. Their tragic dilemma of existence can be better comprehended, if seen in the context of the example of cafe-waiter, which Sartre gives in *Being and Nothingness*. He is not what he appears to be. Sartre says that he is a waiter in 'representation' for others,

> But if I represent myself as him, I am not he, I am as separated from him as the object from the subject, separated by nothing, out this nothing isolates me from him. I cannot be he, I can only play at being him, that is, imagine to myself that I am he. And therefore I affect him with nothingness.[17]

As the waiter is assigned to play a role which is governed by ceremonies, demanding of him, not to nihiliate the state of being he finds himself in, but it is not what it is, i.e. he is not a waiter in the sense a glass is a glass and a table is a table. He is both

In-itself and For-itself. If Richmond Compson is alcoholic and stoic, Caroline is neurotic and whining. Caddy is promiscuous. Jason, a demonic, Quentin an introvert who is obsessed by the horror of the sin of adultery; are they so because they are bound by any set rules or ceremonies? And if it is the moral idealism of the earlier Compsons, which, they think, they cannot uphold, it does not mean that they should start behaving like destroyers of life. Never do they realize that they are not Compsons in the sense a table is a table and a glass is a glass, the consciousness is paralysed, partly by environment and partly by their negativistic attitude to living.

The four Compson children also represent degeneration in varying degree: Benjy is born as an idiot, Caddy is a "fallen" woman, Jason is an amoral materialist, Quentin, the eldest, is alone the Sartoris. He is sent to the University of Harvard to study but, being very sensitive to moral idealism of the earlier generation and puritanical heritage, he cannot overcome the sense or shock, born of Caddy's dishonor and commits suicide which denies him the title of a hero. His father gave him a very pessimistic and anti-human picture of the modern man that "all men are just accumulations, dolls stuffed with saw dust"[18] which he does not believe but cannot rise above it either; of which the self-slaughter is a natural corollary. He is most sensitive to Compson honour, which is why Caddy's adultery becomes an obsession and which even drives him toward self-slaughter. In order to have the stigma of sin faded away, he fabricates the incest theory which his father sets aside as something absurd and unconvincing. As Caddy takes her promiscuity as a protest to set disorder right, Quentin too takes the incestuous desire as a form of order which is, in fact, a vulgar and unheroic form of disorder to make things more problematic. A critic has rightly pointed out that it is an attempt to transform Caddy's amorality of the Snopes world into a sin within the Sartoris morality but the means he employs to do so are pseudo-traditional and romantic, and he fails. Is Caddy's adultery or Quentin's incestuous desire moral? No, certainly not. Rather the truth is that it is the result of the cultural inheritance and partly the moral chaos pervading the family under the shadow of which they grow as destroyers of the finer values of life, Faulkner saw such a free play of wrong value-orientation unleashed around, which is the very source of the fall of aristocracy in the South after the Civil War, history is not used as a myth, but a living reality, rooted in the self-destructive tendencies of the individual characters which Williams Tennessee also uses as a backdrop in *A Streetcar Named Desire* to show that those who could not extricate themselves from the illusion of life on the plantation, were destroyed, Blanche Dubois is a case in point, as against Stella, her sister who survived by accommodating her vision with the changing reality of the 'new economy.'

Benjy is drawn as a Christ image, as against Jason of a Satan. He is invested with an extraordinary mysterious power of sense perception by which he can foresee if some moral disaster has to happen. Thus, he serves as moral reflector for the Compson family. On one occasion we learn, when Benjy sees Caddy carry a bottle of perfume, which is symbolic of the departure from the traditional values, he begins to cry which is gesture of protest, Caddy gives the bottle to Dilsey, saying that it is a gift from Benjy, "We do not like perfume ourselves", Caddy said, and the moral comment comes "She smelled like trees",[19] which is symbolic of purity and natural freshness. If such events of moral implications are reported by someone else, they lose their originality.

Jason is another case who is the 'darling' of his mother and the irony is that he does not need love, nor would return it. He takes delight in tormenting others which is reflected at two places: once, when he burns the two passes in the fire because Luster has no money to buy them and second, when he disfigures Benjy's dolls.

> "He cut up all Beny's dolls." Caddy said. "I'll slit his gizzle."
>
> "Candace." Father said.
>
> "I will." Caddy said. "I will." She fought. Father held her. She kicked at Jason. He rolled into the corner, out of the mirror. Father brought Caddy to the fire. They were all out of the mirror. Only the fire was in it. Like the fire was in a door.

> "Stop that." Father said. "Do you want to make Mother sick in her room."
>
> Caddy stopped. "He cut up all the dolls Mau—Benjy and I made." Caddy said "he did it just for meanness."[20]

Second, his dishonesty is reflected in how he misappropriates Caddy's money which she has been sending every month to support her 17-year-old daughter, Miss Quentin, whom her father, Herbert Head has disowned and deserted and thus she has been living with Caroline. He gives the forged cheques to his mother to burn and keeps the genuine deposited in the bank in his account to invest in stock and support his mistress, Lorraine, in Memphis. But justice is done when one day Quentin breaks into his room, steals money which is her by right and runs way with a carnival man. Jason gives a futile chase and returns home, totally broken and disillusioned. Caroline, the unfeeling and unsympathetic mother, does not take Benjy to the Church, fearing the supposed shame attached to his degeneracy but Dilsey does. The worst that has to befall him at the end is that he is castrated, fearing that he, might molest the girls and is despatched to a mental asylum. What a fine expression of the purity of love, associated with the umbilical ties!

In the midst of the chaos, Dilsey is the only sane voice who represents a unifying and sustaining force to hold the Compson family splinters together. She is For-itself, and has the capacity to change. She is first a human and thereafter someone else, a negro, whose world outlook is not corrupted by bourgeois subjectivism or racial prejudices which is reflected in her taking Benjy to a negro church for Sunday service. When Quentin feels frustrated to learn about good things through the white, he turns to the negroes which suggests his tolerant attitude towards them and which also shows Faulkner's growing awareness of values he discovers in the blacks whom he finds less perverted and in whom he sees no falseness and hypocrisy.

Notes

1. Bill Ashcroft and Pal Ahluwalia (ed.), *Edward Said*, London, New York: Routledge, 2001, p. 58.

2. Hazel Barnes "Special Key to Terminology", in *Being and Nothingness*, New York: Gramercy Books, 1956, p. 632.
3. "The Pursuit of Being", *Being and Nothingness*, p. LXI.
4. *Ibid.*, pp. 617-18.
5. *Ibid.*, pp. 120-21.
6. *Ibid.*, p. 69.
7. William Faulkner, *The Sound and the Fury*, Penguin Books Ltd., p. 73.
8. *Ibid.*, p. 81.
9. *Ibid.*, p. 75.
10. *Ibid.*, p. 90.
11. *Ibid.*, p. 156.
12. *Idem.*
13. *Ibid.*, p. 90.
14. *Ibid.*, pp. 96-97.
15. *Ibid.*, p. 197.
16. *Macbeth* (ed.) Kenneth Muir, London: Methuen & Co. Ltd., 1962, p. 160.
17. *Being and Nothingness*, p. 60.
18. *The Sound and the Fury*, p. 156.
19. *Ibid.*, p. 19.
20. *Ibid.*, p. 64.

Chapter 7

Transcendence as Vision: A Study of Bernard Malamud's *The Assistant*

Malamud's view of man is that of an existential humanist. His works are a searching study in human passions at various levels, seeking to explore the hidden strength of the spirit to show that the inadequacies of life can be sublimated and the 'natural' be humanized, provided man accepts limitations of freedom of self and the territories within which he has to choose to act. Man is a choice-making animal who seeks fulfillment in the act of choosing but it posits certain problems of ontology. Being well aware of the threats of the romantic liberation of self, Malamud shares the view of Martin Buber and Gabriel Marcel who have been the pioneers of interpersonal relations. He is also alive to the ambiguous standpoint of the leading existentialists who, on the one hand, are concerned with the social man, existing as a person in a community of persons but, on the other hand, show concern with the individual's quest for the attainment of an authentic meaningful selfhood.

Malamud's philosophy of life is that of an evolutionary meliorist, he does not believe that evil is insurmountable. This is conveyed by himself, partly in non-fictional writings, articles, interviews, and partly in his novels. During an interview with Haskel Frankel, he has explained the basic idea behind every book:

> My work, all of it, is an idea of dedication to the human. That's basic to every book. If you don't respect man, you cannot respect my work. I'm in defense of the human.[1]

It is this commitment to social aspect of art that takes him to assert Camus' view of art: "The purpose of the writer is to keep civilization from destroying itself."[2] Since Malamud affirms life, he shows his discontentment with the image of man as projected by the contemporary writers, showing him wretched, mean, ignoble, spirituality crippled and morally depraved.

The Assistant is Malamud's very insightful study in how the self becomes aware of the futility of the illusory bohemian pursuits of life and gains realization during the process that freedom is not laissez-faire in morals, rather its essence lies in the concept of interplay of individual freedom and obligations and responsibility and the limits of the freedom of self. It upholds the value of the 'I-Thou' mode of relationship which is based on the proposition that the beauty of living lies in showing concern as much with others as with the self.

The fact is illustrated by what happens to the protagonist who is cast to play an 'assistant' to a saintly Jew.

Malamud chooses the Great Depression of the 30s as a backdrop to show the dehumanizing impact of its resultant evils on human sensibility for want of the consciousness of rational moral choices, which characterize the essence of existence. If the self, instead of preserving purity, chooses self-aggrandizement and acquisitiveness, it suffers from unenlightened moral waverings and is drifted toward a state of nowhereness. The myth is rendered into reality to depict the impact of choices on man, through the two leading characters—Morris Bober, a Jew and his assistant in the title role, Frank Alpine, a Gentile whose struggling self has to scale the alpine moral heights during the process to gain insights into the nature of freedom that it means accommodation, not crushing the other's individuality.

The novel opens in a grocery-store owned by an old Jew, Morris Bober in early November where Frank Alpine, a man from the West, and his would-be assistant, makes his appearance as a gangster. His other two accomplices are Ward Minogue, and the son of detective, Louis Karp, the liquor dealer. Their plan is to rob the store. But his criminality is thawed at the sight of blood on the grocer's head which shows that perhaps Malamud means to project his hero, not as a hardened criminal but having some spark of good within which has been smothered under the shattering burden of wrong choices. Frank is Malamud's extension of his tragic vision, and thus he is drawn—as a creature of natural impulses. As such, if his mind is filled with remorse and guilt at a scene of moral violence, it is at the same time preoccupied with bourgeois evils, such as acquisitiveness, greed, lustfulness and individualism. The place of robbery, they have chosen, does not seem to be a rich establishment, as it is told that the old Jew, despite his battling for the last twenty-one years to overcome poverty has not been able to make any improvement in it. Even he cannot sell it out, being the sole bread earner and, therefore, the Bobers continue to keep living in a five-room flat, the physical condition of which evokes images of cheerlessness.

> The living room was colourless and cramped; for all its over-stuffed furniture of twenty years ago it seemed barren.... Her bedroom was another impossibility, tiny, dark, despite the two by three foot opening in the wall, through which she could see the living room windows.[3]

Ida, his wife complains of poverty, Helen, the only child (their son Ephrain died young), is the worst victim of want and humiliation that has deprived her of means to fulfill any of her cherished desires.

Morris is bound by the store, fated to toil, partly by the design of the book to deflate the bourgeois logic that the moral beauty is a by-product of material prosperity. But the novel is not simple portrayal of misfortunes, despair and gloom the Bobers are subjected to, the real interest lies elsewhere. Could the grisly shadows of Depression rob Morris of his humanity? The storehouse of his strength that keeps up the spirit of strugglesomeness is his faith which is the 'religion of humanity', as Auguste Comte professes, and not in any religious dogma or ritualism. Nor does he, like a rigid religionist, only preach values, rather he lives according to their faith. He could well have chosen to resort to indiscriminate cheatings and dishonest business tactics to amass wealth and tide over the financial stringency rather than preferring to live a life of virtue and die in poverty. When Frank advises him to practice a few business tricks to earn more, such as short-weighing and short-changing, he asks him,

> Why should I steal from my customers? Do they steal from me?... When a man is honest he don't worry when he sleeps. This is more important than to steal a nickel?[4]

The very idea of cheating causes a shudder to keep him close to the vision, as is manifest in his running barefoot in winter to return the balance to a poor Italian lady, she left on the counter, or concealing nothing about the condition of the store from a prospective buyer, Podolsky:

> Overwhelmed by pity for the poor refugee, at what he had in all probability lived through, a man who had sweated blood to save a few brutal dollars, Morris, unable to stand the planned dishonesty, came from behind the counter, and, taking Podolsky by the coat lapels, told him earnestly that the store was run-down but that a boy with his health and strength, with modern methods and a little cash, could build it up in a reasonable time and make a decent living out of it.[5]

Morris does not sustain the illusion of changing the line of business to be rich as one. Julius Karp did and became a rich owner of a liquor shop. He also dismisses the suggestions of a stranger to burn the store and claim money from the Insurance Company saying, "I don't like fires. I don't like monkey business."[6] However, in a mood of dejection, he sets the store on fire, perhaps to free the family from poverty and shame in life in the prison that the store has become. But his apron catches fire and Frank saves him from death.

Morris is an illustration of the idea what Malamud means by the statement, 'all men are Jew.' Morris's idea of a Jew is guided by his father that "to be a Jew, all you need is a good heart.... A Jew must believe in the Law, the Torah." The conversation between Frank and Morris is a rhetorical device to reflect Malamud's own concept of Jewishness which is not characterized by dogmatic ritualism, but by the spirit of the Law that can assure one his humanity before his Jewishness. Morris does not go to the synagogue, he does not eat kosher, nor does he wear black hat which the Law prescribes.

Morris dies of pneumonia as a 'free being', shorn of all whim-whams of life while clearing the snow with a shovel. Malamud brings in other characters as chorus to pin-point the secret of Morris's purity of spirit. The Rabbi's words, he speaks to the mourners on the occasion of his funeral, are significant to show how even the 'unjewish' actions of the grocer could not detract the self from moral promptings and righteousness. He lived like a true Jew, practicing the ideals of doing good to others and enduring suffering heroically with the understanding that suffering is a common lot, which can be mitigated by being as much committed to self as to the community. The Rabbi says,

> There are many ways to be a Jew. So if somebody comes to me and says, "Rabbi, shall we call such a man Jewish who lived and worked among the gentiles and sold them pig meat, trayfe, that we don't eat it, and not once in twenty years comes inside a synagogue, is such a man a Jew, rabbi?" To him I will say, "Yes, Morris Bober was to me a true Jew because he lived in the Jewish experience, which he remembered, and with the Jewish heart." Maybe not to our formal tradition—for this I don't excuse him—but he was true to the spirit of our life—to want for others that which he wants also for himself. He followed the Law which God gave to Moses on Sinai and told him to bring to the people. He suffered, he endured, but with hope. Who told me this? I know. He asked for himself little-nothing, but he wanted for his beloved child a better existence than he had. For such reasons he was a Jew.[7]

Morris is a failure by worldly scale of value, but his weaknesses, in the eyes of the humanists, are the virtues, and the basis of his moral strength that could keep his view of freedom and humanity protected in the neighbourhood which was both corrupt and corrupting in the wake of the eruption of the Great

Depression. Helen also speaks of his virtue and shortcomings which shows his humanity and greatness of soul.

> Papa was honest but what was the good of such honesty if he couldn't exist in this world? He was no saint; he was in a way weak; his only true strength lay in his sweet nature and his understanding. He knew, at least, what was good. And I didn't say he had many friends who admired him. That's the rabbi's invention. People liked him, but who can admire a man passing his life in such a store? He buried himself in it; he didn't have the imagination to know what he was missing. He made himself a victim. He could, with a little more courage, have been more than he was.[8]

Frank is another exemplification of the self in the process of changing. "A man is always changing", Malamud speaks to an interviewer, "and the changed part of his is all important. I refer to the psyche the spirit, the mind, the emotions."[9]

Frank Alpine comes to the east "looking for a better opportunity."[10] His early childhood, in his own words, is a sad story of poverty, deprivation and rootlessness. The sordid heaps of suffering robbed him of the finer sensibilities in life and, as such, the self drifted to marginalization. He felt something missing

> in me, in me or on account of me.... All my life I wanted to accomplish something worthwhile—a thing people will say took a little doing, but I don't. I am too restless—six months in any one place is too much for me. Also I grab at everything too quick—too impatient. I don't do what I have to—that's what I mean. The result is I move into a place with nothing, and I move out with nothing.[11]

Life becomes a nightmare, he fails to understand the meaning of 'pure self' and the ordeals it has to pass through for its purification. He says to Morris: "I don't understand myself. I don't really know what I'm saying to you or why I am saying it."

However, the consciousness of nothingness and absurd reasoning to seek fulfillment is a prelude to the quest for freedom in relation to what it means to be human. He looks back at his own failure and realizes that the sole cause of failure of his aspirations is acquisitiveness and romantic day-dreaming.

> I mean I've been through a lot I've been close to some wonderful things—jobs, for instance, education, women, but close is as far as I go.... Don't ask me why, but sooner or later everything I think is worth having gets away from me in some way or other. I work like a mule for what I want, and just when it looks like I am going to get it I make some kind of a stupid move, and everything that is just about nailed down tight blows up in my face.... I could've been a college graduate by now, but when the time came to start going, I missed out because something else turned up that I took instead. With me one wrong thing leads to another and it ends in a trap. I want the moon so all I get is cheese.[12]

The self is in the process of change to live a life of honesty, sincerity and commitment to its professed ideals but its progress is thwarted by its being incapable to shed evil within. He continues stealing milk and rolls from the store without bringing it to the knowledge of Morris. Why does he not tell the old man the whole story of his pathetic conditions? It is his cowardice or moral hypocrisy to camouflage trickery and deceitfulness? It could be either but certainly the situation is not pleasant as Malamud would have it. Frank's advocacy in self-justification to win sympathy, when caught by Morris, is a travesty of the humanitarian idealism as popularized by the 19th-century European novelists to evoke pity for the victim-hero, who by circumstances became a thief. But no one can lose sight of the fact that evil is self-professed, not forced. Who forced the Arch-angel to choose evil? Adam too as a 'free agent' chose to prefer Eve to paradise to seek self-realisation. The store is Frank's moral paradise wherein the self is to be purged of evil.

Malamud creates opportunities for Frank's moving from romantic egotism to self-discovery. Frank's act of dustering, washing up the windows, and fixing the light in the store is, in symbolic terms, a bid to glistering his evil self. Ida replaces Morris to act as Frank's moral mentor to humanize the waywardness and disorderliness in him. He feels highly embarrassed when the spending money is raised from fifty cents a day to five dollars a week, which shows his growth of progression but this phase of moral compunction is momentary. The manner in which he rationalizes the 'raise': "...it was practically his own dough he was taking", and his continual cheatings ever since the discovery of stealing milk and rolls are the moments of moral waverings and loss of direction.

With Helen's entry into Frank's life, a spectacular change is discernible. As a creature of natural impulses, Frank sets his eye on Helen's beauty to gratify the primeval lecherous passion but at the same time the self is conscious of the dichotomy that any act without owning responsibility will displume it of its real freedom. This restrains him from hankering after her physical assets. There comes a realization as if it were a warning of the self not to feel enamoured of Helen's nakedness in the bathroom, "if you do it, you will suffer."[13] But Frank's moral vacillation, needing transcendence, continues to haunt his imagination, the evil passion seizes over him and he lustily violates the moral dictates of the intellect. The impact of Helen's naked body on the bohemian self is overwhelming:

> He felt a throb of pain at her nakedness, an overwhelming desire to love her, at the same time an awareness of loss, of never having had what he had wanted most....[14]

Frank saves Helen from Ward Minogue's assault on her modesty but lands on her to satisfy the appetite despite her protests. She calls him "Dog-uncircumcised dog."[15] She is willing to condone his non-Jewishness for marriage but now the passionate love degenerates into hatred. After his cataclysmic devilish act of moral violence committed on an innocent, the self is a tortured self, the continuing saintly role suffers from shrinkage; the savior, being drugged by the idea of freedom of its own invention, becomes the destroyer of the morality and value of freedom and wrecks unimaginable agony and violence on the victim. The feelings of self-loathing and stinking carnality rise in a whimper of remorse and repentance: "Oh my God, why did I do it? Why did I do it? Why did I do it?" The spiritual tormentation and the resultant feeling of anguish and pain makes him feel that life has no worthwhile meaning for him. It is not that all is bad as the rise of a sudden 'terrifying insight' shows: "all the while he was acting like he wasn't he was really a man of stern morality."[16] Frank's helplessness to refrain himself from evil that converts the 'free being' into a spiritually crippled being and the flashes of illumination during the act of badness makes him most human. It is this aspect of man as a creature of impulse, opposed to reason, wherein lies the strength of the book.

The determinist would explain Frank's act of moral violence in terms of the Original choice which, it is difficult to determine, whether it was the Original accident or it was willed to be so by the chooser. Malamud is a determinist to the limit that man, if condemned as a puppet in the hands of some inscrutable force, he is, as Heraclitus has said, the maker of his destiny provided his dimensions of freedom are not violated. Frank by his own choice is pushed to nowhereness.

And therefore it is finally after Morris's death that Frank gets another opportunity to feel penitent for his sins and wash out the stigma of being a tramp. He again takes charge of the store, earns the goodwill of the wholesalers to buy grocery items on credit. The self has become alive to the values for which Morris struggled to uphold in life, such as sacrifice, interpersonal responsibility, love and compassion. Now he wants to do something good for Helen, "he could think of no other. All he asked for himself was the privilege of giving her something she couldn't give back."[17] But it is strange that despite invoking God's help to enlighten him as to "why am I killing myself so?" he could find no happy answer and continued spying on Helen to see her disrobe in the bathroom, short-weighted the articles and short-changed the customers. But Malamud writes that one day "for no reason he could give, though the reason felt familiar, he stopped climbing up the air shaft to peek at Helen, and he was honest in the store. With the transformation coming over Frank, Helen's attitude towards him also changes. She realizes that it is for his selfness service to the family that they could keep themselves alive and she could attend night school. The hidden source of change, she feels, is mysterious:

> It came to her that he had changed. It's true, he's not the same man, she said to herself. I should have known by now. She had despised him for the evil he had done, without understanding the why or aftermath, or admitting there could be an end to the bad and a beginning of good.[18]

One day while reading the Bible, Frank imagines St. Francis come dancing out of the woods and take out his wooden rose-flower he carved for Helen. She threw it in the garbage can, suggesting her non-responsiveness in love. But now the flower becomes a real flower in the hands of the saint symbolizing the love between the two that needs proper care for being too delicate. The rose-symbology is a fine illustration of higher truths of life that St. Francis embodied and that Frank's self will have to inculcate to be in the state of self-transcendence. It is further strengthened by his act of circumcision that makes him a Jew, symbolic of his turning to, in broader terms, the religion of humanity and freedom, not in religious sense, though the two are not separate as Sydney Richman points out that "Frank's conversion, like Morris's identity is clearly a humanistic rather than a religious mystery—though two are not necessarily exclusive."[19] In the wake of struggle against evil and the resultant spiritual crisis, Frank's conversion to Jewishness is, in human terms, the moral attestation of his establishing the authentic relationship with the Bobers. In material sense, Frank at the end is left a poor grocer but his struggle has also its spiritual significance to teach him "to want right things" and "to do something big, different."

Notes

1. Haskel Frankel, "Interview with Bernard Malamud", *Saturday Review*, 10 Sept., 1966, p. 40.
2. Quoted in Ihab Hassan, "The Hopes of Man", *New York Times Book Review*, 13, Oct., 1963, p. 5.
3. Bernard Malamud, *The Assistant*, Harmondsworth, Middlesex, England: Penguin Books Ltd., 1957, p. 22.
4. *Ibid.*, p. 78.
5. *Ibid.*, pp. 180-81.
6. *Ibid.*, p. 189.

7. *Ibid.*, p. 203.
8. *Ibid.*, pp. 203-04.
9. Interview with William Kennedy, *The National Observer*, Quoted in W.J. Handy, "The Malamud Hero: A Quest for Existence", *The Fiction of Bernard Malamud.*
10. *The Assistant*, p. 30.
11. *Ibid.*, p. 36.
12. *Ibid.*, pp. 35-36.
13. *Ibid.*, p. 69.
14. *Ibid.*, p. 70.
15. *Ibid.*, p. 151.
16. *Ibid.*, p. 157.
17. *Ibid.*, p. 210.
18. *Ibid.*, p. 215.
19. *Bernard Malamud*, New York: Twayne, 1968, p. 71.

Chapter 8

Treatment of Dream in Arthur Miller's *All My Sons* and *Death of a Salesman*

The paper is an attempt to understand Miller's two plays, *All My Sons* and *Death of a Salesman* in the context of the American dream of success that has its roots, Max Weber demonstrates, in the 17th-century bourgeois England and which was brought to the continent by the Pilgrim Fathers, and was later popularized by the efforts of its interpreters and prophets that one who happens to be in America shall what nothing.

The two protagonists, Joe Keller (*All My Sons*) and Willy Lamon (*Death of a Salesman*), are the personifications of this dream: one is hounded by the American myth of the privacy of the family and is destroyed during the process, while preserving its welfare, by the inordinate vulgar greed for money, the other by his bourgeois adoration of false ideals/values which are wrongly identified with the great American dream in its mythic proportions which ironically subverts the truth of the success ideology.

In *All My Sons*, Miller takes up the theme which is serious and profound in Aristotelian sense for high tragedy: man's fallibility and helplessness to surmount the assault of the basic inner drives in human nature on his moral being, which are common to all and which can strike anyone anywhere in a given situation. The climate, as generated by America's involvement in Vietnam war, was such as necessitated the wholesale manufacturing and supply of the war material to the army during which a class of morally depraved men became alive to smuggle out the fake parts which is as much a bestial crime as to capitalize on war-profiteering.

Miller picks up one, Joe Keller, out of so many Kellers. He runs in partnership a plant where aeroplane parts are manufactured and supplied to the army. He is Everyman in the sense that he has uncritical devotion to the welfare of the family and in enthusiasm commits wrong which is hard for human imagination to conceive of which is smuggling out the fake parts with full consciousness of the horrifying consequences, if they are used. It so happens that one hundred and twenty-one engine cylinders, with cracked heads, are manufactured by a chance defective process. The partner informs Joe all about it and, as morality demand, Joe should have directed him to withhold the supply but he does not do so since it would mean the loss of money. The supply of fake parts in ignorance which is like a fatal flaw to conduct the hero to death, is one thing but doing so knowingly is another. The moment is crucial, Joe has to make a choice which by implication is moral, but he chooses the contrary. He promises to take responsibility on the telephone if there goes some wrong, and asks the partner to ship out the supply and thereafter the real action begins, the crime being already premeditated. Keller suffers from sense of insecurity and makes attempts to keep away the discovery and the doom.

And when the crime is detected, he denies having any knowledge of it in the court and passes the whole blame on to the partner who is sent to jail. As such, he is acquitted but in the eyes of the town people, he is guilty, he is not isolated in the neighbourhood but moves stigmatized as criminal.

The tragic irony comes on the fore when it is learnt that his own son, Larry dies in the crash, cursing the enemy (Joe) who is responsible not only for his but for the death of several flyers. Chris, the second son is rudely shaken by the revelation of this holocaust, signifying 'slaughtering the innocents.' Chris is the 'angry young man', his anger is directed not against one Joe but against America as a whole.

> This is a land of the great big dogs, you don't love a man here, you eat him! That's the principle, the only one we live by—it just happened to kill a few people this time, that's all. The world's that way, how can I

> take it out on him? What sense does that make? This is a zoo, a zoo![1]

Whether the voice is of Chris or Miller's is unnecessary to ask. The feverish rat race for money and man's dehumanization has virtually converted America into a jungle, infested with moral monsters. Chris knows that the wrong cannot be righted and the dead cannot be raised to life, but what is paramount is that at least, Joe can sincerely realise the wrong and surrender to the law which has the power to bring moral transformation and raise the fallen from the state of moral wickedness and depravity to spiritual greatness and retrieve the "rightful position" in the society as Miller would have it. Chris tells his mother to impress upon Joe's mind the moral necessity which is essential to wash out the stigma, the society has tagged on him which she does but the manner in which Joe rationalizes the wrong is a reflection of the ill-conceived myth of the privacy of the family, verging on the crude brutal acquisitiveness, he cannot abdicate the dream.

> Keller: I don't know what you mean! You wanted money, so I made money. What must I be forgiven? You wanted money, didn't you?
>
> Mother: Joe, Joe...it don't excuse it that you did it for family....
>
> Keller: It's got to excuse it!
>
> Mother: There's something bigger than the family to him.
>
> Keller: Nothin' is bigger!
>
> Mother: There is to him.
>
> Keller: There's nothin' he could do that I wouldn't forgive. Because he's my son. Because I'm his father and he's my son.[2]

When Chris questions his humanity asking why he did so, what kind of a man he is who knew that the kids were hanging in the air and did nothing to avert the tragedy, the sixty-one-year old Joe seeks refuge in the age-old bourgeois adoration of the deity, the Business god, at which the boy feels as if put on fire.

Keller: For you, a business for you.

Chris: For me!—I was dying every day and you were killing my boys and you did it for me?

What the hell do you think I was thinking of, the Goddam business?... What the hell do you mean, you did it for me? Don't you have a country? Don't you live in the world? What the hell are you? You're not even an animal, no animal kills his own, what are you? What must I do to you? I ought to tear the tongue out of your mouth, what must I do?[3]

Joe's attempt to exonerate himself from the guilt, holding social system responsible for demoralizing man, "Chris, a man cannot be a Jesus in the world", is a lame excuse. If social system is corrupt, what of Chris? If it were so he would not have been so emotionally hurt to see the father-image collapse he idealises. The feelings of self-loathing rise within.

> I know you're no worse than most men but I thought you were better. I never saw you as a man. I saw you as my father. I can't look at you this way. I can't look at myself.[4]

Larry writes a letter to Annie, the daughter of the business partner the day his plane crashed off the coast of China November twenty-fifth. It is a horrid revelation of human debasement.

The tragic account of the flyers' predicament penetrates deep into Joe's conscience hearing the words of a dying son for a father, he feels as if the very image of being human is slipping away from his fingers. He takes the letter in his hands and looks at it with wild looks in the eyes as if it were Larry striking in the face. In Larry's death, he sees the enormity of the crime, the 'killer of all sons.'

> Then what is this if it isn't telling me? Sure, he was my son. But I think to him they were all my sons! And I guess they were, I guess they were.[5]

The repetition of the words, "I guess they were" is a moral confession of the wrong. It is the tragic insight the classical hero gains. Joe owns responsibility, not only for Larry's death but also for that of all the flyers, whom he calls "all my sons." The 'I-Thou' mode of relationship is established. This sense of social responsibility is further reinforced by what goes off between Chris and Kate. To Kate's question, "What more can we be" Chris' answer is a straightway demystification of the myth between the realm of the private and the public, "I know there is a universe of people outside and you're responsible for it."[6] This is Miller's humanism, the central thesis of the play.

In the meantime, a shot is heard. Joe kills himself, he has illumination, yet he dies the death of a morally corrupt man which, as the orthodox moralists would say, is a just desert for the wrong he perpetrated upon the innocent flyers. The message is plain: there is something higher than self and family, a family is a cognate part of the society and cannot exist in isolation as an island unto itself. What is essential is the acceptance of the principle of interdependence and joint responsibility for the creation of the conditions of living, worthy to be called human. Freedom is no freedom, in case it tends to destroy the "autonomy of moral life" and defile the purity of the earth God created for the men to live on.

Willy Loman (*Salesman*) is an extended image of Joe Keller by virtue of sharing something common: the pursuit of the American dream of success, linked with the myth of the privacy of family and failure, ending in the suicide. Biff's comment in the Requiem-scene that "He had the wrong dreams All, all wrong"[7] and Charley's observation that "Nobody dast blame this man. A salesman got to dream, it comes with the territory"[8], introduce a note of tragic irony: can a little man live upto big issues of life? Is the success myth, by nature elusive, a mirage?

The success ideology which developed a basic outline in the wake of the American expansionism has not been changed since and is still intact (Bernard's success is a case in point); the wrong lies with the confusion of values and the moral pressure it generates upon the pursuer. Miller's statement that 'values do not exist' is vital. What values he points to—the values with which Willy began his career in the early 20s and which have lost their relevance in the post-war business climate which is the time of the play (1948) or the newly emerging values which are expressed in a language the salesman of Willy's generation cannot understand for the simple fact that they are different value—Howard Wagner's values, where the bottomline of profit and loss is everything? Howard is bound by the laws of the modern business morality, according to which 'business is business' which Willy has yet to understand. The act of suicide is taken as a critique of the capitalist America which is why the play was a great success in the communist China, when performed in 1983, with a Chinese cast Miller himself directed. But it is not all. If it were so, then Charley and his son, Bernard would not have been a success story. It is within this framework of value that we have to examine Willy's failure and also pass judgment whether the play is a tragedy of Willy Loman alone or of the salesman culture which is closely tied to capitalism, which is system of power relations as well as exchange relations.

Some hold that it is cultural dissonance, which is responsible for Willy's personal disintegration in the sense that when he practices what he has heard or seen misfires. For example, he has heard the capitalist say that it is humanity as a value, which matters, be it is measured in terms of character or personality. But what of the human appeal he makes to Howard Wagner to accommodate him in the head office as a reward of loyalty of 34 years of service in the Wagner company? He is fired and when he makes a conscience-raising appeal to Howard, "You can't eat the orange and throw the peel away, a man is not a piece of fruit", Howard's words, "Kid, I can't take blood from a stone"[9] virtually render man a commodity, having an exchange value, the moment he ceases to be of any material use for the master whom he has been serving for life, he is thrown out as garbage. Willy's dismissal comes at a very crucial stage when he "has past the point of choice" as Gerald Weales says which cannot be taken in isolation and which posits several overwhelming questions, worth stirring conscience. What when the salesman is no longer marketable? Is the evil remedial, or self-slaughter is the right answer to it?

Willy comes from the American stock that has penchant for travelling and selling. The three salesman figure—the two of the 'Yankee-peddler' tradition, his father and Ben, in the family, the third, Dave Singleman, the 'drummer' are his idols, the success incarnate. His whole life has been shaped by his commitment to the success ideology. There is nothing wrong with the salesman figure but there is every wrong with how he envies their success. In the first place he rejects the traditional values, associated with the early settlers, emphasizing 'character' which Willy lacks. Linda's discussion of Willy's exhaustion which is both physical and moral with the sons is reflection of her humanism but it is also out of truth of what Willy is reduced to in the eyes of the sons, after Biff's encounter with him in the Boston-hotel episode which is the source of the comment "He's got no character."[10]

Willy is thus one evil of the play. He is a symbol of loose morals and so are his sons, he feels happy to know about their 'dating' and advises them not to be serious with the girls in love making.

> No kiddin', Biff, you got a date? Wonderful!... Just wanna be careful with those girls, Biff, that's all. Don't make any promises. No promises of any kind. Because a girl, y'know, they always believe what you tell'em and you're very young, Biff, you're too young to be talking seriously to girls.[11]

One wonders what the boys would learn to grow up with so (fine?) a sermonising on love, amounting to moral perversion in human relations!

The rise of consumerism, and the entry of the middle class into the mass market to own goods which expanded in the wake of the post-war industrial boom made the salesmanship a maddening competition as Willy himself tells "Business is bad, it's murderous." But his denial "But not for me," is a flight from reality which destroys him. It is in this sense that Brenda Murphy rightly calls him "a dinosaur." His placement in the post-war American business world is ill-timed for the fact that the salesman generation of his time was no longer in demand, as against the young men, coming from the war, who had the knowledge of the product and could sell it anywhere to any buyer, after identifying the market.

Charley is also a capitalist and a success by virtue of his adaptation to prevailing business culture which demands of a salesman to have knowledge of the product and service to the consumer. He understands that the business world operates by different laws than human relations. He impresses the same upon Willy's mind, urging him to shed illusion that a man of personal attractiveness "can end with diamonds here on the basis of being-liked" which is traditionally associated with the phrase 'American dream' which he worships without knowing its limitations and promises. What he needs to understand is that what is mythical is not to be confused with what is marketable and that because business has undergone tremendous changes what matter is what one can sell as Charley tells.

> The only thing you got in this world is what you can sell. And the funny thing is that you're a salesman and you do not know that.[12]

This is a blatant statement of reality that simple impressiveness in business no longer remains a value in the post-war American society, which Willy ought to honour but he takes it as an assault on his self-image and spurious tag of sociability he carries around. Knowing that "My New England man" is bleeding, Charley offers Willy a job of fifty dollars a week which he rejects,

> CHARLEY: I offered you a job. You can make fifty dollars a week. And I won't send you on the road.
>
> WILLY: I've got a job.[13]

and chooses to live on the borrowed money to seduce Linda that it is his salary amount. Charley grows impatient, his moral snubbing, "When the hell are you going to grow up?",[14] underlines childish craziness beyond explanation and lack of insight into the dialectic of the success ideology which demands of its pursuer adaptation to the new sales techniques. The problem is, therefore, epistemological as Biff says, "He never knew who he was."

But it is not that Willy is unaware of what is happening to him. He has flashes of illumination of reality as he tells Charley after he is fired "I'm strapped, I'm strapped. I don't know what to do I was just fired."[15] The impact of his dismissal is so devastating as he tells the boys which Miller suggests by evoking the jungle-fire, symbolizing total annihilation, "...the woods are burning boys, you understand. There is a big blaze going on all around. I was fired today."[16] He also tells Linda how people ignore him and laugh at him "and just pass me by. I'm unnoticed." But he does nothing to circumvent the problem which is to jettison the dream and keep dreaming separate from reality, the past from the present. And, moreover, the worst, he does, is that he passes the dream on to his sons, "Be liked and you'll never want", being unaware of its irony that he himself rides on 'shoe-shine' formula and is failing miserably. It is for promoting such a myopic version of the dream that Willy is responsible for their failure, it is not told what happened to them at the end.

Willy cites Ben's story of success to impress upon their mind the importance of industry that "The world is an oyster but you don't crack it open on the mattress"[17] and feels happy to see Ben pat Biff and explain to him the secret of the philosophy of success, "Never fight fair with a stranger, boy, you'll never get out of the jungle that way",[18] which is a philosophy of the dubious morality, amounting to the ruthless exploitation of the natives by the colonizers and 'appropriating wealth by superior weapons.' Second, the education he foists upon them is morally devastating: on the one hand, he wants them to be big in no time, and on the other hand, he does not see thereafter whether they are moving in the right direction. For example, who will appreciate his winking at their petty acts of thievery and bohemian escapades which are hostile to the realization of the dream of success? He calls it 'initiation' and fearlessness, not knowing what Charley warns that "the jails are full of fearlessness characters." This optimism, linked with personality, is self-deception which flows back on his head when in the restaurant where he is invited to a dinner, he is disowned as being their father in the presence of the two 'floozies',

> LETTA: Don't you want to tell your father—
>
> HAPPY: No, that's not my father. He's just a guy. Come on, we'll catch Biff, and honey, we're going to paint this town.[19]

A fine illustration of perversion of human relations.

The father-son confrontation episode in the hotel where Willy is caught with a woman is a fine artistic twist to reflect the moral stature of the salesman but contrary to the philosophy of the success myth which demands of its seeker the quality of character, and honesty in relations. The father image collapses.

Biff: Don't touch me, you liar!

Willy: Apologize for that!

Biff: You fake! You little fake! You fake![20]

The adultery is a direct betrayal of the sacrament, a moral shock to Biff, the discovery of a rubber tube which Willy carries in his room to kill himself is another. Biff is already in a dilemma, because of his own failure in life in the sense that he has not found himself at the age of 34 even on a farm which Willy too calls "a disgrace." What he tells Happy, "I do not know what to do with my life.... I know that all I have done is to waste my life"[21] shows that the magnificence of Willy's star has already faded away.

At last truth breaks in. Biff is already in the process of gaining self-awareness. He has known the limitations of the dream and the system in which Willy is trapped for want of illumination. He will not go by his version of the dream and its promises. He tells Willy that "they never told the truth for ten minutes in the house."[22] It is they who have converted the Loman household into a den of moral hypocrisy and falseness. Willy never let Biff encounter the grim realities of life and thus he holds him responsible for what he has become in life. "And I never got anywhere because you blew me so full of hot air I could not stand taking order from anybody! That's whose fault it is!"[23] He makes confession "Pop! I'm a dime a dozen, and so are you!... I'm not a leader of men.... Pop I'm nothing! I'm nothing! Can't you understand that? I'm just what I'am, that's all."[24] But Willy cannot understand the moral implication of such an outcry of a wounded heart.

Finally, the curtains are drawn. Biff has apprehensions of something sinister to happen in case the dream is not wrapped up. Crying and broken he asks Willy to take "that phoney dream and burn it before something happens." And what Biff fears something to happen, does happen. Linda keeps calling, "Willy, you coming up," and he crashes the car to die the death of a salesman, dreaming of one Dave singleman died. He destroys himself, imagining that Biff will appreciate suicide, out of love as something heroic, a sacrifice to do something for the sons in death what he could not do in life. With the insurance amount Biff will start a business to be big in no time. What a dream!

Biff, after his having an encounter with reality, has lost the will to graduate and join a university, he is overwhelmed by the existential anguish. Thus, in the existing situation whether he will worship Willy for self-slaughter which the scriptures condemn as a sin of purgatory is a matter of anyone's conjecture.

Notes

1. Arthur Miller, *All My Sons*, Philip Reclam Jun, Stuttgart, 2009, p. 118.
2. *Ibid.*, p 112.
3. *Ibid.*, pp. 105-06.
4. *Ibid.*, p. 120.
5. *Ibid.*, p. 122.
6. *Death of a Salesman*, Pearson, 2008, p. 110.
7. *Ibid*, p. 111.
8. *Ibid.*, p. 64.
9. *Ibid.*, p. 43.
10. *Ibid.*, pp. 20-21.
11. *Ibid.*, p. 76.
12. *Idem.*
13. *Idem.*
14. *Idem.*
15. *Ibid.*, p. 28.
16. *Ibid.*, p. 84.
17. *Ibid.*, p. 32.
18. *Ibid.*, p. 38.
19. *Ibid.*, p. 91.
20. *Ibid.*, p. 95.
21. *Ibid.*, p. 104.
22. *Idem.*
23. *Ibid.*, p. 105.
24. *Idem.*

Chapter 9

Feminist Concerns in Tennessee Williams's *A Streetcar Named Desire*

To interpret a work of art from the standpoint of feminist perspective is not different to say what the term 'feminism' implies, what are its leading tenets and how they become manifest in the structural design of the text. As a matter of fact, the movement of feminism is misconstrued from the start that it is a step toward women liberation which prompts a query—liberation from what? The truth is that feminism concerns as much with men as with women, it is a philosophy of coming into understanding between the two sexes how to live as human. To undermine one's individuality, his/her aspirations of life, is a sin of the sacrament.

The feminist consciousness rose in the wake of the 'natural rights doctrine' the benefits of which were denied to women by the male theorists during the Age of Reason which shaped the spirit of the American Declaration of Independence (1776) and the French Revolution (1789). The feminist wanted the same extended to women which was a step toward elimination of gender discrimination. The first wave of feminism is known as the liberal/moderate feminism, the liberals do not favour dismantling the status-quo, their emphasis is on "reform rather than revolutionary changes", they want equal participation and opportunity for women in all sphere of social activities. Contrary to it, the second wave, known as the radical feminism, is violent in its approach to patriarchy. The radicals draw upon the two formulations: (i) that women are oppressed as women and their oppressors are men; (ii) that the distinction between the two is socially constructed, not biological. The system, as governed by patriarchy, cannot be reformed and, therefore, it needs to be "ripped out root and branch." In capitalism, one class is exploited by another, in patriarchy the women, as class, are exploited by men.

The third wave is the socialist feminism, which draws upon the Marxian view of alienation: as workers are alienated in capitalism, women are alienated as women in patriarchy and the reason is materialistic. Therefore, the socialists favour the abolition of property which is at the root of women's subjugation and class hierarchy which encourages class distinction.

The universe of *A Streetcar Named Desire* is patriarchal, men act as the sole master of the house, thereby driving a woman's individuality to marginalization. The feminist concerns in the play are reflected in the treatment meted out to the two Du Bois sisters, who represent the uprooted segment of the Southern aristocracy after the Civil War, when, they were forced to sell out their plantation under the pressure of the 'new economy' to eke out a living. Outside the oppression as unleashed by the patriarchs, Williams shows women, partly responsible for carving out their own hell and heaven. Those who keep fostering illusions of a lost past are driven to disaster, and those, who come to term with reality by accepting facts of existence, survive.

Stella is five years older than her sister Blanche. She is a positive creation who is well aware of the evil consequences of the destructive role of illusions in life. She comes to New Orleans, a cosmopolitan city of easy mingling of the races and marries Stanley, a Polish by nationality, a man below her rank of aristocracy, who is at once a boorish and brute in Blanche's eyes. His other friends, the poker players, are Pablo, Steve, and Mitchell (Mitch), they are all of "heterogeneous types", Morris Freedman rightly points out the hatred of the proletariat class toward the American family pride.

> Stanley Kowalski...scorns the substance and the surface of clean, properly spoken, middle-class American success, scorns the pride that comes with family lineage. Himself

> proud only of his greasy, dirty proletarian work and appearance and speech, his whole bearing a defiance of the usual accoutrements of success, he systematically sets out to destroy the barely flickering spark of family pride, perhaps the only success she has ever known, which sustains Blanche Du Bois, his sister-in-law.

But in the changing circumstances, since the play has a backdrop of the 'plantation myth' as the *Salesman* has the 'success myth', it is reality and realism which, as Williams would have it, must stay. Stella deals with reality in a basically healthy way. If she ignores the needs of others, and eventually adopts her own illusions, it is not cynicism or self-centredness, rather it is something, as the existentialists would say, of utmost value which is suggested by, 'street car named desire' symbology: "Life with Stanley," sex with Stanley is her highest value", Jenne M. McGlinn says.

The scene opens on a street of the New Orleans. The two sisters, Stella who is 25 years old, and Blanche, the elder are discovered. The word 'Blanche' means 'white' signifying 'purity' but underneath, as it is discovered, it is all facade which she exploits and which lands her into an asylum at the end. She is an outsider, a Southern heroine, faded around the edges but still capable of maintaining her 'old-fashioned' morals. Stanley throws a packet of raw meat, symbolizing the gross raw nature, which is a characteristic gesture of overpossessiveness, a patriarchal pride.

> Stanley: (bellowing) Hey there! Stella, baby!
>
> (Stella comes out on the first floor landing, a gentle young woman, about twenty-five, and of a background obviously quite different from her husband's.)
>
> Stella: (mildly) Don't holler at me like that. Hi, Mitch.
>
> Stanley: Catch!
>
> Stella: What?
>
> Stanley: Meat![1]

Blanche comes to stay with Stella but the real purpose is something else—to capture a fly, a man to marry. Her entry is symbolic in the sense that it is she who explains the implication of the title. "They told me to take a street car named Desire, and then transfer to one called Cemeteries and ride six blocks and get off at Elysian Fields."[2] Williams has placed her against Stella and therefore what is interesting is whether she takes the street car as Stella has taken. The treatment meted out to her by the Stanleys is the vulgar display of patriarchal pride. Both Stanley and Stella grow envious of Blanche's costly costumes and suspect that she has squandered their share of money when it is told that the estate of Belle Reve is sold out. The socialist feminists see property as the source of oppression and thus they advocate for its dissolution. Blanche accuses Stella of betraying the family, being unaware of the fact that Stella's existential self has undergone transformation as she tells, "The best I could do was make my own living."

Blanche: I know I know. But you are the one that abandoned Belle Reve, not I! I stayed and fought for it, bled for it, almost died for it!

Stella: Stop this hysterical outburst and tell me what's happened? What do you mean fought and bled? What kind of....

Blanche: I knew you would, Stella. I knew you take this attitude about it.

Stella: About what?—please!

Blanche: (Slowly) The loss-the loss....

Stella: Belle Reve? Lost, is it? No!

Blanche: Yes, Stella.[3]

Blanche's story of the loss of Belle Reve rouses suspicion as the rich jewellery-ridden dresses tell a different story, they take it as Blanche's dishonest dealings who sold out the estate and kept their share by herself.

When Blanche is taking bath, Stanley opens her trunk to examine its contents which is an immoral demonstration of male-egotism and hegemony, Stella urges him to wait but Stanley ignores her implorings and chooses to plunder the wardrobe trunk. He jerks at a fistful of costume jewelry which is sufficient to unnerve a proletarian sensibility.

Stanley: Pearls! Ropes of them! What is this sister of yours, a deep-sea diver? Bracelets of solid gold, too! Where are your pearls and gold bracelets?

Stella: Shhh! Be still, Stanley!

Stanley: And diamonds! A crown for an empress!

Stella: A rhinestone tiara she wore to a costume ball.

Stanley: What's rhinestone?

Stella: Next door to glass.

Stanley: Are you kidding? I have an acquaintance that works in jewelry store. I'll have him in here to make an appraisal of this. Here's your plantation or what was left of it, here!

Stella: You have no idea how stupid and horrid you're being! Now close that trunk before she comes out of the bathroom.[4]

The room where Stanley and his friends play poker is a microcosm of a social order which is organized by men for the advantage of men and wherein the woman's oppression is the law. Men take pride in flying their personal flags in any direction, which is symbolic of their anarchic affirmation of male chauvinism but deny the same to their women. This is manifest in the episode when Stella turns on a radio and Blanche dances to its tune "Wien, Wien, nur due a llien", which Stanley takes an assault on his maleness. He snatches the radio and tosses it out of the window which is certainly brutish because, if Stanley and his friends have right to play poker, the two sisters have also their right to play music.

Stella: Drunk—drunk—animal thing, you! (She rushes through to the poker table). All of you—please go home! If any of two have one spark of decency in you—

Blanche: (wildly) Stella, watch out, he's—

(Stanley charges after Stella)

Men: (feebly) Take it easy, Stanley. Easy, fellow—Let's all—

Stella: You lay your hands on me and I'll—[5]

He does not hesitate even to shower beatings on Stella who is in the advanced stage of pregnancy. Blanche tells Mitch.

> Blanche: My sister is going to have a baby.
>
> Mitch: This is terrible.
>
> Blanche: Lunacy, absolute lunacy!
>
> Mitch: Get him in here, men,
>
> Stella: I want to go away, I want to go away.[6]

and Stanley is pinioned by the two men and is taken into the bedroom as if an hairy ape is thrown into a cage.

This act of violence is no doubt a lunacy for Blanche's aristocratic imagination. She wonders how Stella manages to live with such a man of violent temper. But Stella's image of man is biblical in which man is described as "the provider and the protector" and, therefore, as the moderate feminists are "for reforms, not for revolutionary change," she does not rise in rebellion to raise the protest, thereby to destroy the essence of purity of conjugal bliss. Hers is the philosophy of accommodation and acceptance. She tells Blanche

> I said I am not in anything that I have a desire to get out of. Look at the mess in this room! And those empty bottles! They went through too cases last night! He promised this morning that he was going to quit having these poker parties, but you know how long such a promise is going to keep. Oh, well, it's his pleasure, like mine is movies and bridge. People have got to tolerate each other's habits, I guess.[7]

Another male chauvinistic tendency in man is reflected in Stanley's delving into Blanche's past which is bohemian. He comes to know of how she drove her young homosexual husband, Allan, to suicide and how she was turned out of the school for her bohemianistic pursuits of life, including an affair with a student.

> They kicked her out of that high school before the spring term ended—and I hate to tell you the reason that step was taken! A seventeen year old boy—she'd gotten mixed up with![8]

This discovery is fatal to Blanche's plan to persuade Mitch to marry. Stella arranges a birthday party, in Scene Seven where Mitch is expected to come and their relationship is to take a definite shape. But it is all spoiled by Stanley's perverted self, he tells Mitch all about Blanche's darkening past at which Mitch changes his mind and the poor woman's illusions to marry a man of respectability vanish into nothingness dramatically. Michell (Mitch) is a typical extension of moral ambivalence in his attitude to a women's virginity. Knowing of Blanche's reality he is willing to have relation with her but not to share responsibility the marriage entails. Stanley so brazenly tells Stella all about it. Stella has no idea of Stanley's villainy. She puts twenty-five candles in the cake to give the impression of Blanche being not so old, she expects Mitch to come over the party but what Stanley tells is something sinister that Mitch is not expected to be here tonight.

Stella: Why?

Stanley: Mitch is a buddy of mine. We were in the same outfit together—Two forty-first Engineers. We work in the same plant and now on the same bowling team. You think I could face him if—

Stella: Stanley Kowlski, did you—did you repeat what that—?

Stanley: You're goddam right I told him! I'd have that on my conscience the rest of my life if I knew all that stuff and let my best friend get caught!

Stella: Is Mitch through with her?

Stanley: Wouldn't you be if—?

Stella: I said, Is Mitch through with her?

Stanley: No, I don't think he is necessarily through with her—just wised up!

Stella: Stanley, she thought Mitch was—going to—going to marry her. I was hoping so, too.

Stanley: Well, he's not going to marry her. Maybe he was, but he's not going to jump in a tank with a school of sharks—now![9]

And finally the rape scene is an expression of what Bell Hooks says that "feminism is a struggle to end sexist oppression."[10] Shulamith Firestone in her book, *The Dialectic of Sex,*[11] gives her version of historical materialism, replacing the 'economic class' by 'sex class' and advocate for biological revolution as liberating force but the whole argument seems to be utopian and contrary to the real spirit of feminist ideology. But it is not that Williams supports Stanley's animality, his attitude to man-woman relationship is not shaped by a blatant anti-man agenda, as professed by the radical feminists, he does not endorse Stanley's buffoonery and bestiality. Since feminism is the way of living, a philosophy of life, it urges upon men and women to comprehend its spirit in right way and accommodate their value orientation accordingly to collect its maximum benefits.

Notes

1. Tennessee Williams, *A Streetcar Named Desire*, London: Penguin Groups Ltd., 1974, p. 14.
2. *Ibid.*, p. 3.

   The New Orleans is a cosmopolitan city of intermingling of races. The part of the city, where the action takes place, is named Elysian. Fields which in the Greek mythology is a place to which travelled the warrior heroes after death. But in the play it is not a blessed abode, nor its denizens are heroes, blessed but certainly dead, in a metaphorical sense, for the quality of life they choose to live by.

   It is said that in a Williams's play the focus is on the treatment of the theme of violence and sexuality but it is not all. In the *Streetcar*, the symbolism is enriched by undertones of existential concerns: the 'desire' in the title becomes the driving instinct for life. Each character is obsessed by a desire to live but for want of moderation and restraint he/she is driven to ruination. In case of Blanche, the streetcar named desire becomes one, named Cemeteries, signifying death for her failure to accommodate her view of life with the new view of reality.
3. *Ibid.*, p. 26.
4. *Ibid.*, p. 36.
5. *Ibid.*, p. 57.
6. *Ibid.*, p. 58.

7. *Ibid*., p. 65.
8. *Ibid*., p. 100.
9. *Ibid*., p. 103.
10. Bell Hooks, *Feminist Theory—From Margin to Centre*, UK, Pluto Press, 2000, p. 26.
11. Quoted in Rosemarie Tong, *Feminist Thought: A More Comprehensive Introduction*, University of North Carolina, 2009, p. 74.

Chapter 10

Anti-War American Novels

The American scholar Joseph J. Waldmeir finds the novels of the Second World War, all implicitly, or explicitly, pro-war novels as compared to the novels written about the First War. M. Koreneva disagrees with the critic and says that the novels of James Gould Cozzens, Herman Wouk, R. Powell are "unreservedly pro-war novels" but for different reasons. Instead of exposing the ideological basis of the cruelties of war, its goals and nature, they consider war necessary to affirm and glorify the militaristic ideas. Following the tradition of jingoism, they depict soldiers fighting like gallants, and fearlessly performing acts of heroism whereas the reality is what a Shavian hero demonstrates on the fronts (*Arms and the Man*). Koreneva calls such works inferior, "devoid of any evident ideology but claiming to give an authentic documentary picture of war, are often apologias for violence."[1]

The war novels of Dos Passos and Hemingway are tales of a whole generation, fated to evils as unleashed by a bourgeois society which manifests in the imperialistic character of war on the battlefield. The novels of Norman Mailer, James Jones, John Hersey, Irving Shaw, Mitchell Goodman, Kurt Vonnegut are the realistic war novels in which the writer concedes the necessity of war to strike down an evil which is greater than war itself—fascism. Following the tradition of war novels of the twenties (Dos Passos and Ernest Hemingway) they depict the horrifying consequences of war, its pitiless carnage which brings incalculable physical and moral sufferings to mankind and transforms man into a fanatic, a sadist, a beast. They condemn war as an unjustified mass murder, and it is in this sense that these novels continue to follow the tradition of Dos Passos and Hemingway who write novels using material of the First World War and are not pro but anti-war novels. They are anti-war novels in another sense also which is the exposition of the growing reactionary dangerous tendencies in the American army as supplement to war horrors which threatens to spread from the army into the American society as a whole.

The paper includes a discussion of one novel of the First World War, *A Farewell to Arms* and two of the Second War, *From Here to Eternity* and *Slaughterhouse-Five*.

A Farewell to Arms

A Farewell to Arms is Hemingway's best anti-war novel about First World War, the historical locale, being the year of 1916 when Italy was engaged in war against the Austro-Hungerian Empire in the Alps mountains. The two stories of war and love are fused together in a way that they do not look separate but one to fictionalize the horrors of war and their dehumanizing impact on man.

The protagonist, Henry Frederick, voluntarily joins the Italian army as ambulance driver to have a bitter glory of war and is wounded in the combat zone by a mortar shell. The wound leaves a serious scar on his mind and body. It is not pain but the manner in which the wound is inflicted, a helpless blow from an invisible fist of war machinery.

A Farewell to Arms is different from other war novels in its realistic presentation of the scenes of war, the details do not burden the reader's imagination, nor the reality about the battle scenes is overshadowed. The opening chapter tells about the army-columns, being reduced in scale and size which is symbolic of the very shrinkage of humanity. The scene in which Henry is wounded evokes before us the reality of the situation.

> Though the other noise I heard a cough, then came chuh-chuh chuh-chuh; then there was a flash, as a blast furnace, door is swung open, and a roar that started white and went red and on and on in a rushing wind tried to breathe but my breath would not come and I

> felt myself rush bodily out of myself and out and out and out and all the time bodily in the wind. I went out swiftly, all of myself and I knew I was dead and that it had all been a mistake to think you just died. Then I floated, and instead of going on I myself slide back. I breathed and I was back.[2]

The whole description is much more poignant than war in action, machine gun firing shells, sounds of rifle bullets and explosion of bombs.

The novel is the novelist's insight into human nature, and a profound understanding of the mind of soldiers, their feelings and thoughts. The scene in which one ambulance driver, Passani, discusses war with Henry, before Henry is wounded, is realistic.

> There is nothing worse than war. What is defeat? You go home. They can't do that to everybody. Let everybody defend his home. They can't hang everyone. We in the auto-ambulance cannot even realize at all how bad it is. When people realize how bad it is they cannot do anything to stop it because they go crazy. There are some people who never realize. There are people who are afraid of their officers. It is with them that war is made.[3]

There are scenes in which war brutality is forcefully reiterated at a number of places. The scene in which the dying man's blood drips on Henry's face casts a deadening impact on individual's sensibilities. Henry says, "The drops fell very slowly, as they fall from icicle after the sun has gone."[4] A more brutalizing effect of war is seen during the retreat[5]: the Italian military police take it upon them to try and punish officers and soldiers, who are suspected as deserters. The trial and irrational shooting of the innocents is immoral, they shoot and fling the bodies into the river. Henry's description of the executioners have overtones of irony:

> I saw how their mind worked: if they had minds and if they worked. They were all young men and they were saving their country. The second army was being re-formed beyond the Tagliamento. They were executing officers of the rank of major and above who were

> separated from their troops. They were also dealing summarily with German agitators in Italian uniform. So far they had shot every one they had questioned. The questioners had the beautiful detachment and devotion to stern justice of men dealing in death without being in any danger of it.[6]

Henry escapes by plunging into the river and comes out as a 'new man' who has nothing to do with war. The plunge is symbolic of a kind of baptism which purifies him.

It is war that destroys the conjugal happiness of Henry and Catherine, though their living in togetherness as wife and husband is questioned on moral grounds. Catherine knows that if she is formally married, the authorities would send her away and therefore her self surrender is complete. "But darling, I am married, I'm married to you. Don't I make you a good wife." "You're my religion. You're all I've got."[7] It is a chance that Catherine dies in child birth, not fearing death but with feeling of hatred towards it. "I'm not a bit afraid. It is just a dirty trick." Fate does not give the lovers a chance of enjoying a feeling of parenthood and conjugal happiness. The pathetic quality, so manifest in their final interview, is a reflection of the depth of love.

> "Do you want me to do anything? Can I get you anything?" Catherine smiled. "No", Then a little later,
>
> "You won't do other things with another girl, or say the same things, will you?"
>
> "Never".
>
> "I want you to have girls, though."
>
> "I do not want them."[8]

From Here to Eternity

James Jones's proletariat vision finds expression in *From Here to Eternity*, which is the first of the army trilogy, the other two being *The Thin Red Line* (1962) and *Whistle* (1976), in the creation of a rebellious type of soldiers, like Robert E. Lee Prewitt, the protagonist and Angelo Maggio. James joined the American Air Force in 1939 and confronted the harsh realities of the old pre-World War II army, the officers prospering on caste system and the boy who once was rich but now poor, found it hard to grow in such a harshly regimented existence. The novel deals with America's involvement in World War II. Much of the action of the novel takes place before the Japanese bombed Pearl Harbor on December 7, 1941 and America was not in the military combat. And thus the combat of the two good soldiers, Robert E. Lee Prewitt and Milton Anthony Warden is essentially and paradoxically the combat, not with the enemy but with the army that they serve.

The thirty-years-old Robert E Lee Prewitt (Jones was thirty years old when the *Eternity* was published in 1951) is the son of a miner from Harlon County, Kentucky. During the Great Depression years, the miners of the county were locked into a fierce conflict against the coal operators and to escape the violence and repression let loose on them by the capitalist class. Prewitt represents that oppressed proletariat class in face of the threat to his individuality and man's inhumanity to man.

Prewitt's first shock came during the miners's strike and the treatment meted out to them. His father got multiple stabs and a fractured skull and then imprisonment. It is at this time that Prewitt gave words of promise to his mother on death-bed which later became gospel to forge his conscience. The mother made him take a sacred pledge: "Promise that you would never hurt anybody unless it is absolutely a must, unless you just have to do it."[9]

Jones from the beginning, stresses Prewitt's integrity of belief in ethical imperativeness and honourableness of army as an institution which ironically is destroyed during the process of his growing into soldierhood. He has full faith in the Army regulation and does not want to destroy his own code of integrity. He seems to be hard of the frontier man, the pioneer for whom "words meant what they said."[10] Ihab Hassan also sums up the moral essence of his character: "Prewitt is the perennial collector of injustices, the consecrated underdog. His only code—the simple freedom to be a man, as Prewitt insists—is precisely what the Army he so desperately loves must crush until, still unbroken, he dies."[11]

The book's strength rests on the creation of such characters who, in absence of ideological commitment, show the reactionary tendencies in their conduct and in the guise of democracy espouse fascism to remain in power. It is because of this viper-character of the power-centre that many American war novels denounce democracy with the conviction that democracy rather than fascism is 'the root of all evil.'

Is the stockade episode verging on primitive savagery the reward which the army can give to an honest soldier? Jones himself was never sent to the stockade but he has made the stockade scenes most inhuman and brutal, perhaps to show that it is a replacement of the excesses of the Nazi Germany. Prewitt, at once, becomes conscious of the character of the prison. The clipping shown to him is sufficient to speak of the evil and corruption, existing in the old army as an institution.

> IT WAS SO THOUGH THAT JOHN DILLINGER UPON BEING RELEASED FROM IT SWORE TO HAVE VENGEANCE UPON THE WHOLE UNITED STATES SOMEDAY, EVEN IF IT KILLED HIM. "Beneath this someone has printed: 'which it did.'"[12]

Then Prewitt is introduced to Major Thomson. The truth about him is that he is a devilish character and a dragon. The reality is reflected during the interrogation of the new prisoners. As per ritual, under his direction, they are beaten in the kidney, by the guard with the 'Grub Handles'. Fatso Judson is the first to catch notice of Prewitt during the torture:

> ...S/Sgt. Judson somewhat (resembled) Porky Pig in the Walt Disney Cartoons. S/Sgt. Judson was staring at him with the deadest eyes he had ever seen in a human being. They looked like two beads of caviar spaced far apart on a great white plate.[13]

And Thomson justifies this inhuman brutal Stockade treatment saying that the "quickest, efficientest, least expensive way to educate a man is to make it painful for him when he is wrong the same as with any animal."[14]

What is shocking is that Prewitt happens to see Sgt. Judson killing a man named, Blues Berry. This act of violence is the worst

form of violation of the moral lesson which his mother taught him "never hurting anybody." Here Prewitt's moral idealism is wounded when it confronts the mother's idealism. The only way, Prewitt feels, to right the wrong is killing Judson.

The book's strength rests on ambiguity that gives it the overtone of tragedy as wrought by war on man: Prewitt, does not hate the army, he loves it but the painful paradox is that he cannot surrender his integrity of a soldier to an authority which insists that he should abandon it.

The novel has, therefore, exposed the senselessness of war cruelties. The contemporary war reality destroys the individuality of the soldier and results in the monstrous depersonalization of man. It destroys the romantic individualism and moral idealism. Prewitt is killed, not by a military enemy but as a result of his idealism, colliding against the corruption of the old army, Holmes being the most powerful representative of such corruption. The title *From Here to Eternity* conceals no irony. It closes with the conversation between the boy and his mother. The boy is worried about his future and asks the mother if there would not be any wars left when he grows up and the mother's comforting assurance that he has nothing to fear on that account has its own ambiguity: it goes on, as suggested by Vonnegut's frightening utterance "So it goes." The passion of violence is a reality, man has to shed his fears, egotism, moral pretensions and romantic individualism and evolve a cosmopolitan culture by rising above the petty vulgarities of life.

Slaughterhouse-Five

Kurt Vonnegut, Jr. projects a very pessimistic vision of life in his novels, according to which all human efforts to save mankind from the ravages of time are futile, the dream of socio-economic and political reforms for improving the lot of humanity is rendered meaningless. In *The Sirens of Titan*, Salo, Tralfamadorian 'machine' fails to move his spaceship for lack of a part and thus he is unable to carry on his mission of delivering a message to the inhabitants of various planets. Symbolically, Vonnegut wants to suggest that for the lack of a very minor thing man is unable to continue with his mission and therefore

he is unable to make any improvement in his predicament or to change it. In the words of Josephine Hendine, utter helplessness in the face of overawing situation is the lot of man: "Passivity, acceptance, resignation, and denial are offered as solutions in Vonnegut's novels to the sense of helplessness life engenders." History bears testimony to the fact that man has been struggling for his existence, for a better life and thus he has been trying to discover the inimical forces so as to crush them, though he has been finding this job very hazardous. He has to face various defeats at the hands of cruel forces of history, yet he has never accepted his defeat. But like a typical Black Humourist, Vonnegut would not underline such a heroic character of man. On the contrary, man is "impotent in the face of uncontrollable and untractable circumstances". To quote M. Koreneva, "In Vonnegut's world there can be no transition from suffering to action, from victim to fighter".

Slaughterhouse-Five fully represents Vonnegut's bleak vision of life. It is a novel in which several stories are fused together to give a compact picture of life. Billy Pilgrim's story forms the core of the book in which we see how he feels during the Battle of the Bulge in which the city of Dresden was bombed and what happened to him as a prisoner of war. Another story is related with the experiences of the author himself who was also a prisoner of war.

Vonnegut felt surprised and shocked when Dresden which was supposed to be a very safe city in the whole of Europe was bombed. The city had a few strategic points of military importance and therefore the German authorities assumed that it would not be bombed. But eight hundred English Royal Air Force bombers dropped highly explosive bombs on the city on February 13, 1944 and on the next day American bombers also made a similar attack, on the small city. In this way more than 200,000 people were either killed instantly or died afterward. Vonnegut who was living at this moment along with other prisoners of war in the underground cold-storage area of a slaughterhouse, came out and saw that the whole city was totally destroyed. He was shocked to learn that both the English and the American Governments had ordered to destroy the city because he failed

to understand their purpose behind such an inhuman and callous act. Vonnegut wanted to recapture in a work of fiction the devastating moments of the experiences of catastrophe and with this end in view he tried to gather detailed information about the raid from the Air Force authorities but he was told that the information was still to be classified.

However, Vonnegut did not lose his heart, he met an old friend of his, Bernard V. O'Hare, who had also been a POW with him at Dresden, when O'Hare's wife came to know Vonnegut's plan of writing a book on air attack on Dresden she disapproved of his scheme because she feared that the novelist would glorify war. She told Vonnegut that he (the author) O'Hare and many other men who had been involved in the Second World War were very much like small children. Vonnegut says that war had made her very angry and therefore she did not like that children should be killed in war. Further, she was of the view that books and films on war provided a sort of moral boosting to the war-mongers. Vonnegut tried to dispel her wrong notions when he said that he would sub-title the book as *The Children's Crusade* after the idea floated by two monks in 1213 to recruit children in France and Germany as soldiers for selling them in North Africa.

Vonnegut tells us that destruction has always been a part of life. While staying in a motel, he read various tales of destruction in the Gideon Bible, particularly the passages in Genesis, narrating God raining fire and brimstone on Sodom and Gomorrah and Lot's wife being turned into a pillar of salt when she looked back while she and her husband were running away from the city. Vonnegut draws a parallel between him and Lot and his wife. He says that while looking back at Dresden he has also been turned into a pillar of salt because he has tried to look to the events concerning the bombing of Dresden. Billy Pilgrim has always been a prisoner of war. He had the first experience of war in his early childhood when his father advised him that he should learn to swim by the method of 'sink or swim.' His father wanted to throw Billy in a pool, presuming that Billy would successfully swim. When Billy accompanied his father to the pool and when he found him at the bottom of the pool he lost his consciousness. Even then he felt that somebody was trying to save him. Billy

never got angry at his father for this act of throwing him into the pool or taking him out of it. Since then he has always been willing to sacrifice himself, whatsoever might be the consequences. Josephine Hendine has made a correct estimate of his personality "He is one of Vonnegut's many crucifieds who fight brutally but shutting it out of mind, burying themselves at the bottom of the pool, bottom of the earth, bottom of the universe. Billy does not fight back in war: he gets unstuck in time and space and lets his mind float free."[15]

Billy's getting unstuck in time and space means that feeling shocked at death and destruction is meaningless. Bemoaning the loss of something which was once alive is utter foolishness: we should rather develop a wider concept of time and reject the older one which divides the eternal flow of time into past, present and future. For this purpose, Vonnegut takes Billy to another planet, Tralfamadore whose inhabitants have many novel concepts which are different from those of the human beings inhabiting this earth. A Tralfamadorian explains to Billy the concept of time of his planet which throws light on the limitations of man's vision of life:

> "Earthlings are the great explainers, explaining why this event is structured as it is, telling how other events may be achieved or avoided. I am a Tralfamadorian, seeing all time as you might see a stretch of Rocky Mountains. All time is all time. It does not change. It does not lend itself to warnings or explanations. It simply is. Take it moment by moment, and you will find that we are all, as I've said before, bugs in amber".
>
> "You sound to me as though you don't believe in free will", said Billy Pilgrim.
>
> "If I hadn't spent so much time studying Earthlings", said the Tralfamadorian, "I wouldn't have any idea what was meant by 'free will', "I've visited thirty-one inhabited plants in the universe, and I have studied reports on one hundred more. Only on Earth is there any talk of free will."[16]

This fascinating account of Tralfamadorian concept of time has enlightened Billy to gain a great insight into the mystery of life and death. For him death is not a horrifying event because when a person dies he only appears to die. And therefore we should accept death as the universal truth and say to ourselves, that such an inevitable event has always been taking place and will go on taking place in future also.

> The most important thing I learned on Tralfamadore was that when a person dies he only appears to die. He is still very much alive in the past, so it is very silly for people to cry at his funeral. All, moments, past, present and future, always have existed, always will exist. The Tralfamadorians can look at all the different moments just that way we can look at a stretch of the Rocky Mountains, for instance. They can see how permanent all the moments are, and they can look at any moment that interests them. It is just an illusion we have here on Earth that one moment follows another one, like beads on a string, and that once a moment is gone it is gone forever.
>
> When a Tralfamadoria sees a corpse, all he thinks is that the dead person is in a bad condition in that particular moment, but that the same person is just fine in plenty or other moments. Now, when I myself hear that somebody is dead, I simply shrug and say what the Tralfamadorians say about dead people, which is "so it goes."[17]

In the light of this newly-discovered truth, Billy concludes that all moments exist simultaneously and therefore we cannot change either the past or the future because, as a matter of fact, past or present does not exist. As a result, Billy feels that man does not have a free will and therefore he is very much satisfied to accept the message inscribed on the locket worn by Montana Wildhack:

> God grant me the serenity to accept the things,
> I cannot change, courage to change the things
> I can, and wisdom always to tell the difference.[18]

What does this imaginary travel of Billy to Tralfamadore imply? Billy is unable to do anything worthwhile to understand why man has to face such ravages as war (or why he refuses to know the facts responsible for such ravages like economic interest of the nations following capitalistic or imperialist path of social development), he has to invent some psychological justification for his inaction or state of inertia. For such a man and his creator like Vonnegut, James Lundoquist observes, that what they do is nothing but an effort "to re-invent themselves and their universe to come up with some new lies so they go on living."[19] About Billy the critic has rightly said: "Billy is unhinged to the point of madness by what happens to him in war, and he can on longer control his time tripping, so he invents the Tralfamadorians to make his madness accord with some vision of reality. His life is thus given a certain order and pattern and he does attain serenity."[20] Even Vonnegut has developed a similar dispassionate attitude towards death. "When I think about my own death, I do not console myself with the idea that my descendants and my books and all that will live on. Anybody with any sense knows that the whole solar system will go up like a celluloid collar by-and-by I honestly believe, though, that we are wrong to think that moments go away never to be seen again. This moment and every moment last for ever."[21]

Nevertheless, consciously or unconsciously, Vonnegut expresses his disgust with war and condemns it, he is also critical of the American society for keeping the vast majority of people as victims of poverty. Referring to the American involvement in Vietnam War, Vonnegut narrates what a major observes on the issue. We cannot miss the sarcastic digging at America's continuing war in the poor but valiant country:

> Americans had no choice but to keep fighting in Vietnam until they achieved victory or until the Communists realized that they could not force their way of life on weak countries. The major had been there on two separate tours of duty. He told of many terrible and many wonderful things he had seen. He was in favor of increased bombings, of bombing North Vietnam back into the Stone Age, if it refused to see reason.[22]

But Billy, the mouthpiece of the author, remains detached to what is happening in Vietnam. Perhaps Vonnegut has all of a sudden become conscious of the stance of indifferent characteristics of a Black Humourist. He observes:

> Billy was not moved to protest the bombing of North Vietnam, did not shudder about the hideous things he himself had seen bombing do.[23]

Vonnegut's laconic utterence 'So it goes' suggests horror of war. War will never end unless man controls the beast in him. Billy feels himself utterly helpless in the face of this lived reality and thus he develops an outlook of cynicism.

> "So it goes."
>
> "It had to be done," Rumfoord told Billy, speaking of the destruction of Dresden,
>
> "I know", said Billy.
>
> "That's war".
>
> "I know, I'm not complaining".
>
> "It must have been hell on the ground".
>
> "It was", said Billy Pilgrim.
>
> "Pity the men who had to do it".
>
> "I do."
>
> "You must have had mixed feelings, there on the ground."
>
> "It was, all right", said Billy. "Everything is all right, and everybody has to do exactly what he does. I learned that on Tralfamadore."[24]

After some time Billy is again overwhelmed by cruelty wrought on man by man. In reply to a question posed by a Tralfamadorian he narrates some events of cruelty and callousness and concludes that he fears the war may escalate in other planets also:

> As you know, I am from a planet that has been engaged in, senseless slaughter since the beginning of time. I myself have seen the bodies of school girls who were boiled alive in a water tower by my own countrymen, who were proud of fighting pure evil at the time. This

> was true. Billy saw the boiled bodies in Dresden. And I have lit my way in a prison at night with candles from the fat of human beings who were butchered by the brothers and fathers of those school girls who were boiled. Earthlings must be the terrors of the Universe! If other planets aren't now in danger from Earth, they soon will be. So tell me the secret so I can take it back to Earth and save us all. How can a planet live at peace?[25]

How the Earthlings, a Tralfamadorian sanely explains, may learn to live with a sense of growing menace as caused by the nuclear weapons which man himself invented to blow up, not only the planet he inhabits, but rather the other planets in the universe as well.

> "Would—would you mind telling me", he said to the guide, much deflated, "what was so stupid about that?"
>
> "We know how the Universe ends," said the guide, "and Earth has nothing to do with it, except that it gets wiped out, too." "How—how does the Universe end?" said Billy.
>
> "We blow it up, experimenting with new fuels for our flying saucers. A Tralfamadorian test pilot presses a starter button, and the whole Universe disappears." So it goes. "If you know this," said Billy, "isn't there some way you can prevent it? Can't you keep the pilot from pressing the button?"
>
> "He has always pressed it, and he always will. We always let him and we always will let him. The moment is structured that way."
>
> "So," said Billy gropingly, "I suppose that the idea of preventing war on Earth is stupid, too."
>
> "Of course."
>
> "But you do have a peaceful planet here."
>
> "Today we do. On other days we have wars as horrible as any you've ever seen or read about. There isn't anything we can do about them, so we simply don't look at them. We ignore them. We spend eternity looking at

> pleasant moments—like today at the zoo. Isn't this a nice moment?"
>
> "Yes".
>
> "That's one thing Earthlings might learn to do, if they tried hard enough: Ignore the awful times, and concentrate on the good ones." "Um," said Billy Pilgrim.[26]

Howard W. Campbell, Jr., a well-known American playwright, has described in a monograph of his that paradox of American nation: America, on the one hand, is the wealthiest nation in the world but, on the other hand, its people are poor. He also comments that many beliefs of the Americans are based on false foundations, one of them, being that "it is very easy for any American to make money."[27] Campbell further remarks that the rich and wealthy people do not care to do anything for the poor.

But mere casual comments on the problems of poverty and war and the like without analysing the root cause of the malaise will be of no avail. Josephine Hendine aptly comments that Vonnegut seems to be telling us "to go dead to the fact that the past is the destruction you have known, the present the violence you see, and the future the holocaust to come."[28]

Notes

1. M. Koreneva, "The Contemporary War Novel", *20th Century American Literature: A Soviet View*, Moscow: Progress Publishers, 1976, p. 50.
2. *A Farewell to Arms*, pp. 53-54.
3. *Ibid.*, p. 47.
4. *Ibid.*, p. 46.
5. *Ibid.*, p. 168.
6. *Ibid.*, p. 174.
7. *Ibid.*, p. 104.
8. *Ibid.*, p. 136.
9. *From Here to Eternity*, New York: Charles Scribner's Sons, 1951, p. 16.
10. The comment was made in John Dos Passos's *USA*, Harmondsworth, 1966, p. 353.

11. Ihab Hassan, *Radical Innocence: The Contemporary American Novel*, Princeton, New Jersey: Princeton University Press, 1973, p. 84.
12. *From Here to Eternity*, p. 532.
13. *Ibid.*, p. 535.
14. *Ibid.*, p. 534.
15. Josephine Hendine, "Experimental Fiction", *Harvard Guide to Contemporary American Fiction*, Oxford University Press, 1979, p. 259.
16. *Slaughterhouse-Five,* London: Granada Publishing Ltd., 1972, p. 61.
17. *Ibid.*, p. 25.
18. *Ibid.*, p. 139.
19. James Lundoquist, *Kurt Vonnegut*, New York: Fredrick Ungar Publishing Co, 1977, pp. 52-53.
20. *Ibid.*, p. 139.
21. *Wamgeters, Foma and Gransfalloons*, New York: Delta, 1975, p. 258.
22. *Ibid.*, p. 45.
23. *Ibid.*, p. 46.
24. *Slaughterhouse-Five*, p. 132.
25. *Ibid.*, p. 80.
26. *Ibid.*, pp. 80-81.
27. *Ibid.*, p. 89.
28. "Experimental Fiction", *Harvard Guide to American Fiction, op. cit.*, p. 239.

Chapter 11

Contemporary Black Humour American Novels: From Nathanael West to Thomas Berger

The paper is an attempt to understand the genesis of Black Humour and the reason why, in spite of its failure to present a cogent vision of life and treating the serious too lightly and comically, the writers in the West, particularly the novelists, felt attracted towards this movement, discovering in its aesthetics a new tone to fit into the recent American fiction, it also includes the discussion of a few works of its leading practitioners, beginning with Nathanael West, a novelist of the 30s to the post-war novelists, such as John Barth, Thomas Pynchon, Joseph Heller, Kurt Vonnegut, Thomas Berger and Walker Perey. And since Andre Breton developed the concept of Black Humour from the Surrealistic disgust with the canons of value, and Surrealism being an offshoot of Dadaism, the two ultra-modern movements are discussed within as much limitations as are found fitting into the argument, not in detail, for want of space.

The term 'humor noir', the English translation of which is 'black humour' appears in Andre Breton's *Anthology de L humour noir* (1939), from France the term reached England but altogether in a different form and finally the *Time* magazine published an article in 1965 on the American novelists, entitled "The Black Humourists" which was the official attestation of the term, thereby becoming currency in literary critical jargon. Defining its philosophical formulations into a few words is a balancing feat, partly for its showing affinity with and departure from the other contemporary movements, like the Theatre of the Absurd, Existentialism, the Angry Young Men and the Beat Generation movement. For example, sometimes a Black Humour protagonist is confused with a Beatnik for betraying anarchically individualistic and bohemian tendencies in human conduct to the extent that the absurd world looks more absurd and fragmented in the hands of the Black Humour novelists who are interested more in justifying the illusion of supremacy of their artistic imagination which is nothing but a device of distancing art from the real life situations and its ironies, rather than arming man with means needed to come to terms with life to live by that we see in the works of the positive singers of the Absurd, Camus' *The Myth of Sisyphus*, being a class illustration.

Even Bruce Jay Friedman who edited an anthology *Black Humour*, himself claims to have no clear conclusive definition of the term, he says that "it is, as hard to define black humour as to define an elbow or a corned beef sandwich." Taking into consideration Friedman's metaphor 'corned beef sandwich', Donald J. Greiner observes that Black Humour is a protean term and attempts to define it are difficult. However, he suggests a viable definition of Black Humour:

> ...it makes no attempt to minimize the terror of the post-World War I universe; it uses comedy to encourage sympathy as well as to expose evil it suggests futurity; it celebrates comic distortion as an indication that anything is possible; and it is related to the poetic use of language.[1]

There could be three responses to face up the absurdity and meaninglessness of human existence: first, that there are left no absolute values to guide the course of human destiny, and accept the facts of existence as they are and thus exploit like a cynic this state of valuelessness to overcome the stress of the time; second, to stage withdrawal in despair and develop a nihilistic view of life; third, to assume a stance of defiant laughter, as the final human response. In other words, to mock scornfully at the absurd situations in life, including the serious. In a Greek theatre, the spectator is brought face-to-face with larger issues of life, concerning human predicament. Can the laughter of a

Black Humourist be a human response to make sense out of the senselessness of human condition in a universe that remains silent to the call of the human for clarity?

Sarah Blacker Cohen agrees with Max F. Schulz that the Black Humour is a product of the 'sixties' but it owes its debt to the writings of a band of writers who are designated as the sick comedians of the 'fifties' for reflecting in their writings a sickening vision of life. She calls them the progenitors of Black Humour who appeared to

> serve as the lunatic commentators of our collective lunacy, a role they assumed with a vengeance...they joked about H-bomb fall out, neo-Nazism, failed Russian-American détente.... Upholding no ethical norm, they censured for the perverse delight of censuring.[2]

But soon they lost appeal for being so outrageous in that treatment of mockery and excessive nihilism that the audience "became surfeited with their invective. No longer appreciated the sick comedians, either self-destructed or vanished."[3]

Continuing the above tradition of criticism of the sickening treatment of life, Kenneth Allsop observes that these comedians "gouge the customers where they are most sensitively vulnerable, insult them to their wincing faces, and nightly implant unease that the barbecue pit is the abyss."[4]

Mary Allen, too considers Black Humour writings as purely a 'sixties-affair', though its hilarities can be traced back in antiquity: "A general term for much of the writing of the 'sixties' is black humor, a concept difficult to define, of long-standing use in literature, which entails a comic-revulsive reaction to things grotesque."[5] An anthology, entitled *Black Humour* (1972) includes writings only of the black writers which removes its generic confusion that Black Humour has any affinity with the black colour.

However, contemporary movement of Black Humour in American fiction owes its origin to Andre Breton's Surrealism which is an offshoot of Dadaism. Dada was a group of nihilists who flourished as literary and cultural rebels in the heat of the First World War which proved the bankruptcy of a whole intellectual, cultural and social systems because rationality and religious and human values were slaughtered by the so-called civilized nations. All the illusions about the real world were destroyed during the war years—faith in traditional moral and religious feelings, usefulness of science and the worth of intellectual were shattered. The adherents of Dadaism averred that Dadaism could be a record of the contemporary catastrophes, the announcement of the failure of cherished ideals and the death of an age-long civilization. In this way, this movement was not only skeptical of everything holy and ideal, but it was a philosophy of total negation.

Tristan Tzara, the founding father of the movement, declared, that "measured by scale of eternity, any activity is futile." His further observation on the Dadaist wholesale destruction and utter negativistic tendencies is pertinent.

> We spite on humanity. ...Dada is the abolition of all logic. There is a great negative work of destruction to be done. We must sweep everything away and sweep clean.[6]

Andre Breton found everything quite insignificant: Georges Ribemont Dessaignes considered that the sense of discrimination between the beautiful and the ugly was also useless. Dadaists believed that it was quite ridiculous to make any effort at distinguishing the true from the false or the right from the wrong because nothing could be contradicted.

During these years, Einstein's theory of relativity bewildered the absolutists who could no more support the idea of objective truth. However, these rebels did not yield to the pressure of conformity in the social, cultural and political institutions. Andre Breton declared in his *Confession Le'daigreuse*,

> Absolutely incapable of resigning myself to any lot, wounded in my highest conscience by the denial of justice which in my eyes original sin does not excuse at all, I shall not adapt my existence to the absurd conditions of all existence in this world.[7]

This tone of individual revolt of Andre Breton was actually a romantic distrust of institutionalized faith which is reflected in their condemnatory verdict on literature. Even the best literature is mere imitation of the writings of great masters, they said, and, therefore, if an artist wants to know himself, he will have to break his own ground. So they preferred spontaneity and authenticity of a felt experience. This emphasis on individual experience of truth led them to the study of Freud's rejection of the conscious and the search for the truth in the unconscious and the subconscious. The Dadaists had their own notion about the job of an artist and the role he had to play in creating a work of art. To Jacques Riviere the job of an artist is as follows:

> To grasp our beings before it has yielded to consistency, to seize it in its incoherence, or better, in its primitive coherence, before the idea of contradiction has appeared and, compelled it to reduce and construct itself; to replace its logical unity, which can only be acquired by its absurd unity, which alone is innate.[8]

Surrealism (its period is marked between the two World Wars) is a further extension of the major philosophical foundations of Dadaism which made, says Hans Richter, Dadaists surrealists overnight. Like the Dadaist, the Surrealists, in the first place, were also non-conformists which is manifest in their revolt against social norms, and intellectual and moral values, they rejected the concept of rationality as propagated by the bourgeois ideological formulations and put everything to cruel vivisection. The term 'Surrealism' coined by the French poet made its appearance in Guillaume Apollinaire's play, *Las Memelles de Tirisias* performed in 1917 to convey the sense of essential reality but the true spiritual background of the movement may be traced back to Rimbaud, Lautreamount, the German Romantics and the Symbolists. Its goal is announced in its famous periodical, *La Revolution Surrealistic*.

> Abandon the Caves of being. Come. Reason wafts outside reason. The time has come to part with your dwelling places.... Ideas, logic, order, Truth (with a capital T). Reason.... We consign them all to the oblivion of death. Preserve your logics, gentleman, preserve your logics; you cannot imagine to what our hatred of logic may lead us.[9]

Albert Camus defined Surrealism in the following words:

> Absolute rebellion, total insubordination on principle, the humour and cult of the absurd—such is the nature of Surrealism, which defines itself in its primary intent as the incessant examination of all values.[10]

His further comment on Surrealism clearly underlines its relationship with Freudian concept of the unconscious.

> The instinctive joy of being alive, the stimulus of the unconscious, the cry of irrational, are the only pure truths that must be professed. Everything that stands in the way of desire—principally society—must, therefore, be mercilessly destroyed.[11]

This emphasis on the indomitable individuality of man obliged the Surrealists to draw upon the Romantics for the ethics of love. They adored primitive instincts and impulses at the cost of rationality and reason and relied upon revolutionary measures to preserve their ideals. In this connection they sought the help of Marxian concept of revolutionary overthrow of burgeois institutions. For sometime they supported the Bolshevik cause of the liberation of the proletariat and the establishment of a communitarian society. But they were not prepared to sacrifice their inner self to any political doctrine of institution. Breton announced,

> All of us see to shift power from the hands of the bourgeoisie to those of the proletariat. Meanwhile, it is nonetheless necessary that the experiments of inner life continue and do so, of course, without external or even Marxist control.[12]

Thus, it is evident that the attempt of Surrealists to synthesise romantic individualism and Marxian communitarianism was an exercise in futility because, in the words of Eugene Goodheart, they tended to affirm "indomitable egotism." Anna Balakian rightly calls it "promethean individualism."[13]

From these premises of surrealistic disguist with the established canons of values, Breton developed his concept of Black Humour. According to him, humour is a means of defending the inner self against,

> constraints of human condition, physical and psychological as well as social. "...Humour enabled one to transcend the trivial reality in which man is imprisoned by logic, reason and subjective emotion, freeing him to achieve union with the objective metaphysical Absolute. Detached by humour from the culturally determined self, man's dark unconscious could express its metaphysical yearnings and inhibitions in the form of untrammelled dream, fantasy and nonsense."[14]

Black Humour disturbed because it was not necessarily nor always "light-hearted, funny, amusing, laughter-provoking... it violates sacred and secular taboos alike without restraint or compunction."[15] It discovered its cause for laughter in what had been generally regarded too serious for frivolity, for example, disease, physical deformity, mental disorder, pain, suffering, anguish, terror, decay and degeneration of institutions and death. It avoided sentimentality with coolness of mind and preferred the tactics of surprise and shock and in doing so, it negated the importance of emotions and sentiments and violated the eternal values of life such as love, kindness, sympathy for the victims of pain and suffering and the importance of sacrifice for the sake of certain basic principles of life because it had no faith in the eternity of anything. In face of the holocausts of war and the collapse of culture and civilization, the Western intellectuals looked at it as the only psychic remonstrance against the fear of nuclear devastation, the onslaught of political bossism and bureaucratization of institutions on the mind of helpless people.

Such a negative attitude ceased to be a sincere condemnation of a value-structure when it did not provide a strategy of fighting against disvalues and adopted merely the artistic tactics of surprise and shock "with absolutely no intention of attempting to reform the human foibles and vices that it castigated", and therefore it became "a kind of corrosive ridicule of human behaviour, so negative in tone and destructive in its effect as to constitute satire for its own sake."[16]

Nathanael West is the first major American writer of the 1930s to be considerably fascinated by the philosophy of Black

Humour. The novelistic canvas as painted by West, in the words of Grigson Geoffrey, projects such a world as looks like a "desert of panic and emptiness and his books mercilessly analyse the human condition." The mode of comedy, West employs, is black, violent and grotesque and in his novel he dramatizes the American dream of liberty and the pursuit of happiness being turned into an illusion by corrupting and destroying means of a selfish society. Each novel of West, to quote Max F. Schulz, exposes the emptiness and falsity of a coveted dream: the bardic dream, for example, in *The Dream Life of Balso Snell* (1931); the Christ dream in *Miss Lonelyhearts* (1933); the Horatio Alger dream in *A Cool Million* (1934) and the Hollywood dream in *The Day of the Locust* (1939). About the horse which symbolizes falsity and end of a civilization Schulz comments that the "thorough-going nature of his (West) sense of the fraudulence and destruction of life is brilliantly, almost excessively, portrayed by the Trojan Horse correlative in *The Dream Life of Balso Snell*."[17]

The protagonist of the novel, undertakes a long journey in the alimentary canal of a wooden horse through which West satirizes cultural values and age-long tradition of morality and flings into air the Western intellectual and artistic accomplishments. Against the setting of the American dream paradise Hollywood, which has been painted by West as a nightmarish place of cheap hotels, of love turning to lust, boredom, fading illusions, violence and mob-riots, *The Day of the Locust* exposes vulgarity and lustful violence prevalent in American society, Lemuel Pitkins, the hero of *A Cool Million* sets out to make his fortune in the land of opportunity but he is robbed, beaten up and assassinated and thus the capitalistic slogan of honesty and hard labour as the only way to make great progress sounds hollow and empty. The life, West portrays in his novels, strikes a "conflict of inadequate imperatives offered to man by society and culture as guides to live by."[18]

John Barth's *The Floating Opera* (1956) shows its concern with modern dilemma of value. Barth, like other Black Humourists, projects man's bohemian outlook on life and rejects all moral norms and essence of intrinsic values of life, such as love, fellow-feeling, sense of dedication and sacrifice. The 'floating opera' is used as a symbol of life: life, like the floating opera, Barth demonstrates, presents a show of broken episodes which make reality too difficult to comprehend. "Nothing has intrinsic value", Todd Andrews, the narrator protagonist of the novel, speaks and if nothing has value, "there is then, no reason for living" and thus he decided to kill himself one morning. Therefore, the novel deals with the problem of suicide but the real tone of the book is caught in the end when Todd rejects his self-styled value of suicide and decides to live stating—"If nothing makes any final difference, that fact makes no final difference either, and there is no more reason to commit suicide, say, than not to in the last analysis."[19] Thus, Todd rejects absolute values and prefers relative values but he does not explain what those relative values would be. Schulz's observation in this regard is pertinent here: "This conception of its protagonist the common man *manqué* is what makes Black Humour a somewhat limited vision, capable of the specific aberrations of comedy, rather than the universal condition of tragedy."

It is sheer stroke of chance that the three novels of Thomas Pynchon were published within this decade (his *V* appeared in 1963 and exactly after ten years in 1973, he broke silence by publishing *The Gravity's Rainbow*). Pynchon's heroes fight against the impersonal hostile forces which threaten human progress and growth of society. In *The Crying of Lot-49* (1966), Oedipa Mass embarks on a quest to interpret the text of the will of her former rich lover, Pierce Inverarity. Pynchon describes the strange world of San Narciso in which nothing is natural, everything is designed to have a purpose of its own. Oedipa Mass becomes a victim of insanity; when she comes down to Los Angeles, she finds the object of her quest the Tristero empire mystery not easy for her to unravel. In the end, the text, which she set out to interpret, turns out to be the legacy of America itself.

Many novelists have drawn force of their fictional universe and dark comic vision from their experiences in World War II. Prominent among such novelists are Kurt Vonnegut and Heller. Heller's *Catch-22* is a powerful attack on the dehumanizing military bureaucracy and U.S. entrepreneurial greed. Heller introduces a new figure into post-war American fiction who throughout the entire novel invents reasons for staying out of air and avoiding flying missions, instead of fighting the war. Yossarian's stance of indifference which is a central characteristic of Black Humour fiction is a powerful condemnation of the "imperialistic character of war which openly ignores the interest of humanity in the pursuit of business."[20] M. Koreneva justifies Yossarian's obstinacy by quoting dialogue between him and his head, Major Danby. The Major romanticizes war glory and advises him to "look up at the big picture" to which Yossarian replies: "When I look up, I see people cashing in. I do not see heaven or saints or angels. I see people cashing in on every decent impulse and every human tragedy."[21]

The tinge of Black Humour in all its aspects is carried over to the writings of science-fiction, notably in Vonnegut. Vonnegut projects in his novel a dark vision of life, asserting his viewpoint that all efforts to improve the lot of mankind are meaningless. The universe as depicted in science-fiction is one without God and human beings are presented as highly advanced mechanical creatures aspiring to be God by demolishing old comforting illusions about the logical conceptions. Such an absurd universe is a fitting target of Black Humour satire. In *Cat's Cradle*, for example, Vonnegut ridicules the idea of 'truth' of science and religion and concludes that mankind is "better off living by "foma" or harmless untruths. *Slaughterhouse-Five* is Vonnegut's scathing attack on man's love of war, a translation of the reality of fire-bombing into fiction. It is a characteristic novel of Black Humour in which the protagonist, allegorically named Billy Pilgrim, "is set down in a world that kills and maims in the most casual and summary way."[22]

Thomas Berger's *Vital Parts* (1970) is the final novel of a trilogy, the first two being *Crazy in Berlin* (1958) and *Reinhart in Love* (1961). Carlo Reinhart is the central character through which the thematic continuity is conveniently maintained. He struggles to keep his conscience alive "amid vital incongruities of post-war America" but on account of his ultimate failures he is ironically reduced to the level of an "innocent fool, jocular lover, mock hero and death defier."[23] His *Little Big Man* (1974) is a serious parody that issues from the contrast between myths that have clustered around Western value structure and its reality.

Notes

1. Foreword *to Black Humour*, New York: Bantem Books, 1965, pp. vii-viii.
2. Sarah Blacher Cohen, "Introduction: The Variety of Humours", *Comic Relief: Humour in Contemporary American Literature*, Urbana, Chicago: University of Illinois Press, 1978, p. 2.
3. *Ibid.*, pp. 3-4.
4. "Those American Sicknicks", *The Twentieth Century*, July, 1961, p. 98.
5. *The Necessary Blankness: Women in Major American Fiction*, Chicago, London: University of Illinois Press, 1976, p. 6.
6. Mathew Josephson, *Life Among the Surrealists* (A Memoir), New York: Holt, Rinehart and Winston, 1962, p. 110.
7. Quoted in Marcel Raymond, "Dada", Irving Howe (ed.), *Literary Modernism*, Greenwich, Connecticut: Fawcett Publications, Inc., 1967, p. 205.
8. *Ibid.*, p. 207.
9. Quoted by A. Kukarin, *The Passing Age: The Ideology and Culture of the Late Bourgeois Epoch, op. cit.*, p. 303.
10. "Surrealism", Irving Howe (ed.), *Literary Modernism, op. cit.*, p. 212.
11. *Idem.*
12. Quoted by Eugene Goodheart, *Culture and the Radical Conscience*, Cambridge: Harvard University Press, 1973, p. 139.
13. *Idem.*
14. Brom Weber, "The Mode of Black Humour", in *The Comic Imagination in American Literature*, New Brunswick, New Jersey: Rutgers University Press, 1973, p. 265.
15. *Ibid.*, p. 266.
16. Rod W. Horton and Herbert W. Edwards, *Background of American Literary Thought*, London: Prentice Hall Inc., 1974, p. 594.
17. *The Concise Encyclopedia of Modern World Literature*, London: Hutchinson and Co-Publishers Ltd., 1963, p. 381.

18. *Radical Sophistication: Studies in Contemporary Jewish American Novelists*; Ohio: Ohio University Press, 1969, p. 37.
19. *Idem.*
20. John Barth, *The Floating Opera*, New York: Doubleday and Company, Inc., 1967, p. 270.
21. *Black Humour Fiction of the Sixties*, Athens, Ohio: Ohio University Press, 1974, pp. 10-11.
22. Joseph Heller, *Catch-22*, London: Gorgi Books, 1961, p. 469.
23. Morris Dickestein, "Black Humour and History: Fiction in the Sixties", *Partisan Review*, Vol. XLIII, No. 2. 1976, p. 205.

Chapter 12

Robert Frost's 'Birches'[1]—An Appraisal

Frost's poetic philosophies are a by-product of a paradox—the confrontation between the ideal and the real but the boundaries of the two do not lose their separateness for the fact that what he sees of life as "a bursting unity of opposites", the same he puts into his principles of aesthetics and art and therefore it is the acceptance of the ultimate reality as its stands which cannot be divorced from the ideal, rather it heightens its nature. This dichotomy between the ideal and the real pervades Frost's entire poetical universe.

Second, it is often said that in a Frost-poem there is no resolution and if there is any it is larded with symbolic overtones which creates confusion. He takes one or the other problem as confronted by the modern man and leaves its tangles unresolved which is hardly fair. The truth is that there is a resolution, a direction which is clearly marked in his poems, provided one takes pain to probe deeper into its layers of meaning, keeping in mind what he said that "a poem begins in delight and ends in wisdom."[2]

What Frost said that "poetry is a metaphor"[3] saying one thing and meaning another, finds full explication in the poem 'Birches' which runs into 60 lines, falling into three divisions and embodying one of Frost's major themes. Frost's view of poetry is that poetry is "clarification of life"[4] by which he means that poetry deals with a meaning which may clarify how the mingled goodness and badness of life is to be accepted as the ultimate philosophy of life to live: growing too much optimistic over the existence of one and too much pessimistic over the other is not the ideal as Frost would have it, what is needed is the avoidance of the extremes. This is Frost's answer to those who ask in what measure poetry is a "clarification of life."

The poem 'Birches' is a fine blend of observation and imagination. It begins with the description of the birch trees in a very easy conversational tone which is one characteristic feature of Frost's poetry.

> When I see birches bend to left and right
> Across the lines of straighter darker trees.[5]

One can easily come across a very common sight of the trees in New England, growing both sides of the walk, and bending their branches downward toward the ground. Fancy comes in about the phenomenon that perhaps some boy who is out to graze cattle must have done it by swinging on them. But soon he corrects himself that it cannot be the doing of the boy because the trees can go to their original posture when released. When "Truth breaks in with all her matter of fact" that it is the ice storms that have dragged them down and taken out the stiffness, he says that "swinging does not bend them down to stay/ Ice storms do that." The two beautiful images are introduced in which there is a fine interplay of fact and fancy. The first image is built on the phenomenon, occurring in nature which is hardly to be contradicted. On a sunny winter morning after the rain, the snow crust load on the trees cracks with the rise of the winds and falls down which looks like a heap of glass to the speaker's fancy. It is a fine poetic exaggeration but the total meaning is conveyed.

> They click upon themselves
> As the breeze rises, and turn many-coloured
> As the stir cracks and crazes their enamel
> Soon the sun's warmth makes them shed crystal shells
> Shattering and avalanching on the snowcrust—
> Such heaps of broken glass to sweep away
> You'd think the inner dome of heaven had fallen.[6]

John O'Hara calls the image of ice, looking like a heap of glass whimsical in that it arrests the reader's attention without warning for a change of tone when facts turn into fancy.

In the second image, the poet sees the trees in a new way, they are humanized in that they are transformed into girls when they are bending forward on their knees to dry hair.

> You may see their trunks arching in the words
> Years afterwards, trailing their leaves on the ground
> Like girls on hands and knees that throw their hair
> Before them over their heads to dry in the sun.[7]

The tree trunks trailing their leaves on the ground build a complete picture of human activity.

The first section ends in line 22 with the factual phenomenon about the trees and the source of the bend. Now from line 23 onward, the poet's imagination takes wings, he says that he is "free to the poetical?" but the real purpose that the poem purports to convey is not overshadowed by flights of fancy. He wishes some boy bend the trees while he is grazing cows and, being single, play the game of climbing the tree in what the poet sees a prolonged process of moral elevation.

> I should prefer to have some boy bend them
> As he went out and in to fetch the cows.[8]

Unlike other boys who are fond of playing baseball with their fellows, this boy who is fond of swinging the birch trees, loves to be left alone in his game. He seeks delight in the game by means of his own efforts and plays about, be it summer or winter.

> Some boy too far from town to learn baseball,
> Whose only play was what he found himself,
> Summer or winter, and could play alone.
> One by one he subdued his father's plays.
> By riding them down over and over again
> Until he took the stiffness out of them,
> And not one but hung limp, not one was left
> For him to conquer.[9]

'Heaven' is a recurrent word in Frost's poetry, most often it is a substitute for the sky. But here in the poem it metaphorically suggests some imagined state of perfect bliss, some ideal human attitude of life. Frost uses imagery of a cup, which is already full of water upto the brim and to add more water to it is difficult, a balancing feat which is linked with the work-ethics to attain perfection in life. The boy is an expert swinger, the poet says, who has learnt all that there is to learn how to reach the top carefully, fearing fall and then launching out, carrying the trees to the ground.

> He always kept his poise
> To the top branches, climbing carefully
> With the same pains you use to fill a cup
> Upto the brim, and even above the brim.
> Then he flung outward, feet first, with a swish,
> Kicking his way down through the air to the ground.[10]

And here ends the second section which runs for 23-41 lines. In the third section, the poem becomes rather philosophical. The act of 'climbing' and 'coming down' are symbolically interpreted: 'climbing' is symbolic of man's quest for higher spiritual values and aspirations of life, one has to maintain a poise, a calm and patience while learning to acquire these higher values, and 'coming down' means their translation into practice to moralize nature in the midst of humanity. Climbing in this sense in a ladder of quest and setting feet down on the ground with the trees is a tangible suggestion of putting into practice the acquired wisdom of life. The poet sees in the act of climbing a silver lining as a guide to enable man surmount the confusion of values in life. The poet says that once he himself was a swinger and wishes to be one again. The reason he explains, is less metaphysical and more existential. It so happens that when the mind is assailed by doubts, confusion, perplexities and vexations of life, it longs for an escape, to seek clarity and illumination. The poet, as human, feels depressed by fever and fret of life. It is in these moments of confusion and weariness that he thinks of cutting himself off from the sight of human spectacle of pain and misery by being a swinger of the birches temporarily. He sees life as a 'pathless wood', where walking is painful, the 'cobwebs' strike the face and the open eye weeps. Dorothy Parker calls it a 'temporary suicide.'

But is the escape lasting? No, it is not. The poet wants to come back to the earth to live and seek fulfillment in earthly values. If Fate misunderstands him and grants half of what he desires, it is a great misfortune, he says

> May no fate willfully misunderstand me
> And half grant what I wish and snatch me away
> Not to return.[11]

The poet has an intense longing for life which can be realized on earth.

> Earth's the right place for love:
> I don't know where it's likely to go better.[12]

It is a call for the celebration of earthly glories and values; earth is the place assigned by God to man to attain the ideal and beyond it is all trespassing. The last two lines

> That would be good both going and coming back
> One could do worse than be a swinger of birches.[13]

lift the poem from the mundane sphere of day-to-day, human activities. Thomson's understanding of the central idea is worth quoting: "one might not to do violence to 'Birches' by discovery in the final passage a reflection of the poetic hunger for withdrawal which might permit swift and exciting, return with grace and without effort to a new sense of life."

The 'Birches' is thus one of the characteristic poems of Frost which enriches one's understanding and outlook on life to come closer to vision. The two situations are contradictory but otherwise illuminating. 'Climbing' symbolizes acquiring wisdom of life of which one is deprived in case he is not a swinger and 'coming back' is putting the acquired wisdom into practice for the practical use in life. The higher truths of life which the swinger learns during the upward assent, are to be shared by mankind as a whole. This is Frost's humanism.

Notes

1. The poem "Birches", Louis Untermeyer rightly points out, is one of Frost's most widely-quoted poems which beautifully illustrates the poet's power of blending observation and imagination. It first appeared in the *Atlantic Magazine* in 1915, and was later published in the volume "Mountain Interval", New York: Henry Holt, 1916. The citations are taken from the Penguin edition.

2. In "The Figure a Poem Makes", Frost explains how a poem, by stages, evolves into being which constitutes the basis of his theory of poetry: What the poem clarifies as 'something' is the wisdom of life.

   It begins in delight and ends in wisdom.... It assumes direction with the first line laid down, It runs a course of lucky events, and ends in a clarification of life.

   Hyde Cox and Edward Contlery Lathem, eds. *Selected Prose of Robert Frost*, N.Y.: Holt Rinehart & Winston, 1966, p. 18.

3. Robert Frost, "The Constant Symbol", in *Selected Prose of Robert Frost*, *op. cit.* p. 24.

   There are many things I have found myself saying about poetry, but the chiefest of these is that it is a 'metaphor', saying one thing, and meaning another, saying one thing in terms of another.... Poetry is simply made of metaphors. Every poem is a new metaphor inside, or it is nothing. And there is a sense in which all poems are the same old metaphors.

4. Quoted in George W. Nitchie, *Human Values in the Poetry of Robert Frost*, Durham NC: Duke University Press, 1966, p. 210.

   The strength of the statement that the poetry is "a clarification of life", or "a momentary stay against confusion" rests on the principle of creation by means of which what appears at first in day-to-day life the inexplicable and the hazy, becomes at the end intelligible and lucid.

   Frost's statement that "A poem is an arrest of disorder" is also its powerful endorsement.

   Out of chaotic confusions and daily impressions and thoughts, the poet captures a moment with the words and achieves a kind of crystallization that gives his chaotic raw materials, not only shape, but weight.

   Frost has also said elsewhere that the making of the poem is a chance creation, but his emphasis on the value of affirmative resolutions, and clarification of life in poetry is never overshadowed.

   ...a poet is essentially an accidental collector of impressions and knowledge, that the making of a poem is largely a matter of trusting to luck, a poem's logic is backward in retrospect after the act, the reality a poem touches is chaos. From the contact with that reality, the poem may produce, if he is lucky, a clarification of life, not necessarily a great clarification, such as sects and cults are founded on...but a momentary stay against confusion.

   Lawrence Thompson, Frost's biographer, has made a fine analysis of the poem, "West Running Brook", to explain what 'clarification of life' in poetry implies. The brook's flow westward and of the others toward the east "to catch the ocean", brings to the poet's mind the very analogy of existence, which shows that life, as the poet sees, is "a bursting unity of opposites", and the need is to seek reconciliation between the disparate and the irreconciliables. The best poetry, the critic contends, touches on the realms of the spiritual values where in the mundane and the ephemeral gets transcended.

Poetry deals with a meaning and truth which may clarify the mingled goodness and badness of life without growing too optimistic over the existence of one and too pessimistic over the existence of the other. And these overtones of significance implicit in the poem are permissible as subject matter for cannotation on that higher plane of poetry." This is Frost's simple answer to those who ask in what measure the poetry becomes "a clarification of life".

5. Ian Hamilton, ed. *Robert Frost: Selected Poems*, Penguin Books Ltd., 1975, pp 80-81, lines 1-2.
6. *Ibid*., lines 7-13.
7. *Ibid*., lines 17-20.
8. *Ibid*., lines 24-25.
9. *Ibid*., lines 26-33.
10. *Ibid*., lines 36-41.
11. *Ibid*., lines 51-53.
12. *Ibid*., lines 53-54.

    The two situations, getting 'away from earth a while', suggesting a growing sense of dissatisfaction with life, and declaring Earth at the same time as being 'the right place for love', signifying an intense longing for life on earth, are highly paradoxical: the two things cannot go together but because both are realities, the human realities, they are to be accepted and somehow to be lived by. The act of 'climbing' is not escapism, as Frost himself has said, "Well, a man may climb a tree and still not be an escapist. He may go up there to pluck something.... There is always something else in my poetry." And that 'something', Reginald L. Cook says, is the "old intuitive knowledge and the simple truths of human hearts," which one has to learn to seek balance between the disparate forces of affirmation and negation which is one of Frost's major themes. This is the wisdom, the poem ends with, the poet professes. Elizabeth Jennings has also made a very wise observation on this ambivalence pervading in art and life: that "coming down" is the poet's "preference for the immediate tangible world and his ability to manage without too much consideration of transcendental things."
13. *Ibid*., lines 59-60.

Chapter 13

The Beat Generation and James Patrick Donleavy

The paper attempts to dismantle certain misconceptions that have clustered around Donleavy-criticism and provide a correct assessment of his vision of life, as explicated and exemplified in his novels and short stories.

It is a matter of great regret that except a few casual remarks about Donleavy's individual novels, no full length study of any of his novels or plays has been attempted so far. And if we peruse the extant critical material on the author, it shocks us awfully. Almost all the critics hold that Donleavy is a bohemian who propagates the individualistic ideals of barbaric primitive sexual anarchy and revolt against moral, religious and social norms. In this connection, they believe that Donleavy is a spokesman of the Black Humour and the Beat Generation, whereas the fact is that he satirizes the evils of these movements by dramatizing the horrifying consequences of the immoral and inhuman action and vulgar manners of his egocentric and acquisitive characters, who indulge in whoring and drinking. While doing so, Donleavy shows that his protagonists start their horrible adventurous journey, presuming that the fulfillment of their lust for wealth and sex is the ultimate goal of life but eventually they realize the futility of their illusory hope. During and after the long period of their bewildering odyssey, they are isolated from their friends, family and humanity at large, and consequently they begin to hate the very value-orientation of the bourgeois society which favours such an acquisitive outlook and perverts intrinsic human values.

Thus starts the process of their redemption, but it is too late for them to regain their lost energy and the real happiness of life. Therefore, they suffer from an acute awareness of emotional crisis and psychological breakdown. In this way, Donleavy indicts and protests against the bohemian ways of life like the Absurdists and the Angry Young Men. For presenting heart rending, pitiable conditions of his protagonists, Donleavy dexterously uses the artistic devices of irony, satire, farce, sarcasm and symbolism which most of the critics have failed to appreciate, on the contrary, they have identified his protagonists' outlook with their creator's in a bid to establish their viewpoint that he is a champion of the ideals of the Black Humour and the Beat Generation.

For example, commenting on Sebestian Dangerfield (*The Ginger Man*), the *Time Magazine* observed: "Donleavy turns the moral universe on its head by making the reader love Dangerfield for his killer instinct, flamboyant charm, wit, flashing generosity—and above all for his wild fierce, two-handed grab for every precious second of life." Similarly, The Irish Press commented: "...morals are mocked at and indecency is flaunted."[1]

Continuing the above tradition of the criticism of Donleavy's works, most of the critics and reviewers call him a Black Humorist, while other critics have lumped him with the Angry Young Men. Still others consider him as a link between the Angry Young Men and the Beat Generation. Perhaps Jerry H. Bryant believes that Sebestian Dangerfield is a typical apostle of the Best Generation who, by his conviction and actions, is trying to formulate a new code of morality. Moreover, there are other critics who observe in Donleavy's works only wit, fun, humour and fantastic inventiveness. For example, Granville Hicks remarks that Donleavy's writing is "distinguished by humour often inelegant, even coarse, but explosive and irrestible."

There is an another school of critics which explains his comic vision shrouded with a sense of existential dilemma. Max F. Schultz comments that Donleavy is a "uniquely modern Aristophanist with an existential horror of death", while Gerald Weales argues that the "peace" which Sebestian pursues with such demonic energy is death. Dean Cohen, finds *The Ginger*

Man, "a terrifying fable of man's course through life in progress from danger to danger until he is finally devoured." T. LeClair, too, discovers a dying process: "novels are obsessively concerned with death."

Let us see what are the founding principles of the philosophy of the Beat Generation and how Donleavy shows departure from them by satirizing their phoney quest which, they say, is religious.

The movement of the Beat Generation which started gaining momentum at the end of the 'fifties' was another exploration in the possibility of restoring individual dignity, which verged on unrestrained individualism. The protagonists of the movement were critical of the whole socio-economic, political and intellectual traditions of the West. They were horrified at the horror of the Second World War and condemned the technocratic cultural revolution that was taking place around them because they found the impact of this culture on human sensibility to be more disastrous than the modern political upheavals. Commenting upon the evils of the modern technocratic cultural revolution, David McReynolds rightly remarked that the contemporary man has lost his identity and his sense of belonging to his family and community:

> This is a revolution that subjects society to constant and shattering changing. There are no stable institutions to which, the individual can turn. The son cannot follow his father's trade even if he wants to, for technology destroys old trades one day and creates new ones the next. Cultural patterns are eroded by a system of mass production and mass communication in which we all become like one another, speaking the same language, wearing the same clothes, reading the same magazines. But instead of creating a sense of community, this only creates a crowd of faceless and anonymous men.
>
> How is a man to know who he is today? By what does he identify himself? Not by a relationship to the soil on which he was born—for we have left the land for the city, where we flit like harried vagrants from one apartment to another. Nor can a person find his identity

> in the family—for that institution is breaking down. By winning the right to enter the labor market women have found a degree of economic freedom that makes a marriage less necessary—our high divorce rate is one price we pay for technological progress. The sudden equality of the sexes creates tension in both men and women as they realize that their old roles are destroyed but are uncertain what their new ones should be.
>
> This is the society of the mass. We know everyone by his first name—trying to imply a relationship which does not exist. Families living in an apartment house are more isolated from their neighbors a few feet away than were families on the American frontier who lived twenty miles apart. The individual is never able to feel that he is an important part of some meaningful whole. Our hearts ache with loneliness but we do not know how to talk to one another. 'Society' is a word from which all content has been drained. Society doesn't mean community—there is no community, only what David Reisman calls 'the lonely crowd.'[2]

Reynolds also pointed out that the contemporary world is devoid of all basic moral values. "Words like 'freedom' and 'peace' became 'masks'," he said, "for conformity and violence and the death of individual spontaneity."[3] He disapproved of Russians' and Americans' claim of being defenders of peace and democracy because, according to him, the individual does not enjoy freedom, either in Russia or America. He criticized America's role in world politics, "...the concern for freedom is betrayed by the United States in precisely those areas where it has power to make the ideal a reality. In Algeria, it supplies the French with NATO arms. In Formosa, it overlooks the tyranny of Chiang Kai Shek over the native population. In Latin America, it supported Batista and supplied him with military equipment until he was overthrown. The ultimate expression of America's disregard for any concept of 'truth' was contained in those statements of the Administration favouring nuclear tests in order 'to give humanity a clean Hydrogen Bomb'. Youth senses intuitively that a set of relative 'values', which not only permits but demands the building of hydrogen bombs and guided missiles, is not a set of values at all, but a rationale for insanity."[4]

Commenting upon such a state of affairs in politics and its impact upon art, literature and morality, John Clellon Holmes, the prominent spokesman of the Beat Generation, observed: "Conventional notions of private and public morality have been steadily atrophied in the last ten or fifteen years by the exposure of treason in government, corruption in labor and business, and scandal among the mighty of Broadway and Hollywood. The political faiths which sometimes seem to justify slaughter have become steadily less appealing as slaughter has reached proportions that stagger even the mathematical mind. Orthodox religious conceptions of good and evil seem increasingly inadequate to explain a world of science-fiction turned fact, past-enemies turned bosom-friends and honourable diplomacy turned brink-of-war. Older generations may be distressed or cynical or apathetic about this world, or they may have somehow adjusted their conceptions to it."[5]

Being thrown in such an inhuman world, Holmes declared that the Beat Generation "cannot conceive of the question in any but personal terms and knows that the only answer it can accept will come out of the dark night of the individual soul."[6] He championed the cause of the "affirmation of an individuality... which can sometimes only be expressed by outright eccentricity"[7] in "the removal of every society and intellectual restraint to the expression and employment of his unique individuality and in the creative power of the unfettered soul."[8]

For such a seeker of individual freedom, society became its deadliest enemy against which every individual member of the Beat Generation revolted. In order to maintain their individuality, the members of the Beat Generation resorted to acts of delinquency, promiscuous sexual relations, drug addiction and loved jazz music. Herbert Gold, another important spokesman of this generation, prescribed the use of narcotics to the members of the generation because "the more than anything gives Little Boy Beat what he wants—release from imagination and the body—an illusion not of Omnipotence, but of a timeless browsing in eternity."[9]

The single question the Beat Generation seems to be occupied with is—how are we to live?—which is existential in conception but the manner in which the beatniks resolve this question is highly comical, verging on naked primitive individualism which is morally destructive to primeval mode of collective existence: "The hipster would propose a program which would be the removal of every social and intellectual restraint to the expression and enjoyment of his unique individuality."[10]

Norman Podhoretz says that the source of the rise of the Beat Generation lies in the intellectual impoverishment as well as hostility to the intellect

> ...the Beat Generation's worship of primitivism and spontaneity is more than a cover for hostility to intelligence; it arises from a pathetic poverty of feeling as well. The hipsters and hipster-lovers of the Beat Generation are rebels, all right, but not against anything so sociological and historical as the middle class or capitalism or even respectability. This is the revolt of the spiritually underprivileged and the crippled of soul—young men who can't think straight and hate anyone who can; young men who can't get outside the morass of self....[11]

The "rebel" is called 'hypster' and the movement as American existentialism which finds its manifestation in the cult of hypsterism, which, in its worship of spontaneity and action against 'conformity', and the hipster in his rebellion against the contemporary 'chaos', tends to be delusory for want of any moral direction, as some critics have said that "these wild young hedonists were not really representative of anything but were only "freeks", "mental and moral imbeciles", "bourgeois rebels".

Norman Mailer, a major novelist who enriched the philosophy of this movement, exhorted his compatriots to go back to the state of primitive barbarism in which sex would not be and taboo and violence would be considered a source of potential creative energy. He found totalitarianism in the popular art, the social craft, the political craft and the corporate techniques,"[12] in medicine, architecture, technology and mass media of America.

"The essence of totalitarianism," he said, "beheads individuality, vanity, dissent, extreme possibility, romantic faith, it blinds vision, deadens instincts, it obliterates the past;" it creates a sort of cancer "which is not a disease, but a loss of self."[13] His fascination for individualism became apparent in his concept of Hipsterism/ American Existentialism. Fearing the danger of conformity and depression he suggested to prefer "to accept the terms of death, to live with death as immediate danger, to divorce oneself from society, to exist without roots, to set out on that unchartered journey into the rebellious imperatives of the self."[14] His ideal self became Hip who he equated with a Negro because both fear that their life is in danger, and that their ultimate goal of life is the pleasures of the body. Hipster is, he said, "the sophistification of the wise primitive in a giant jungle:"[15] he is a psychopath who "murders...out of the necessity to purge his violence."[16] Pleading his cult of violence, he said that killing one's adversary is "an old religion, a more primitive one."[17] His views on sex are not less challenging: "God which every Hipster believes is located in the senses of his body:" it is "the unachievable whisper of mystery within the sex."[18] As a spokesman of the "absolute sexual freedom", he tried to reinstate the lost glory of the instinct and save the "animal in us" from extinction.[19] He did not hesitate to justify even homosexuality and rape. His craze for individual freedom reached its apogee when he said that Hip "abdicates from any conventional moral responsibility,"[20] and asserted that man should divorce himself from his values and liberate himself from the superego of society because "the only Hip morality... is to do what one feels whenever it is possible" and therefore Hip should make efforts "to open the limits of the possible for oneself, for oneself alone because that one's need."[21] And lastly, "His...is the affirmation of the barbarism."[22]

From the above analysis, it is evident that the members of the Beat Generation are wild bohemians whose only aim of life is to live on the plane of animalistic sensuality. For example, the characters of Jack Kerouac in *On the Road* go to New York, Denver and San Fransisco in search of sexual pleasure for making their life happy. In their journey from one place to another, they buy and steel cars, hitch hike and ride a bus; they listen to Jazz and sleep with beautiful girls. Their craze for indulging in sexual and sensual orgies is reflected in Sal Paradise's comments: "The only people for me are the mad ones, the ones who are mad to live, mad to talk, mad to be saved, desirous of everything at the same time, the ones who never yawn or say a commonplace thing, but burn, burn, burn, like fabulous yellow Roman candles exploding like spiders across the stars."[23]

Though the propounders of the movement of the Beat Generation claim to have developed a viable philosophy of life, no sane person can accept their claim. Carolyn Gaiser makes an apt comment in this context. "The Beat movement cannot really be classified as a philosophy since it is not a rational position arrived at through a cool intellectual analysis of the human condition. Nor is it in any sense political. Though poems may be written about evils of "The Bomb", there are no prescriptions for altering the government or re-structuring society."[24] Nor do they have any political philosophy in their minds to redress the evils of the contemporary world. In the words of Bernard Duffey, "They came not to replace one political or moral scheme with another, but to deny all such systems in favour of apparent anarchy. The Beats would not so much destroy society and its values as simply disaffiliate, and once free, begin a quest for some reality, but one governed only by individual existence."[25]

A look into his works shows how Donleavy rejects the rebellion of these "Know-Nothing Bohemians" and recommends, by implications, a philosophy to live life fully and live it in a proper way.

His first novel, *The Ginger Man,* exposes the evils of individualism such as acquisitiveness, lustfulness, sex without love and the resultant perversion of human relations, which have devoured the elemental values in the West. People suffering from these evils consider that the value-orientation, they have developed on the basis of their vile pursuits is the ideal vision of life and, therefore, they violate the canons of basic values, such as love and marital fidelity in a bid to fulfill their illusory, aspirations. But, ironically enough, they eventually become victims of their wrong-directed value-orientation—they are isolated from the mainstream of life, from their family, friends, and community, and their life becomes quite unbearable.

The acquisitiveness of the protagonist, Sebastian Balfe Dangerfield, drives his wife, Marion, the daughter of a retired English admiral, away from him and, thereafter, he becomes intimate with a number of girls, Christine, Lily Frost and Mary Maloney who play a foul game to widen the gulf between Sebastian and Marian. Christine says, "I wonder if there is any such thing as a perfect sex life among married people"[26] which is a hint that sexual pleasure can be had only in extramarital relations. Sebastian also supports her view and says that love between husband and wife "waxes and wanes"[27] which shows that they both support debauchery. Donleavy exposes the beastliness of Sebastian and Christine and the nakedness and vulgarity governing the lifestyle of the Beats.

Justifying Sebastian's seduction of Miss Frost, Jerry H. Bryant says: "His violence and venom...contribute, as Donleavy would have it, to the creation of new life." "Sebastian is justified," he says further, "in defiantly violation a stuffy society's most cherished values: familial devotion, marital fidelity, ambition, respect for property and money."[28]

His friend 'O' Keefe is another symbol of sexual perversion and moral depravity in the West. He is a victim of poverty and fails to get human love and indulges in drinking and homosexuality. In a letter to Sebastian, he writes: "I am destined to love beautiful women and to inspire in them a desire to lay for someone else—My homosexual personality is complete. I have been reading André Gide in French, the Marquis De sade a Casanova. It's just like they say it is being in love with a boy—No more women—I've discovered I'm impotent, ejaculatio praecox."[29] He does not find any joy or happiness in life and is driven to utter loneliness. He goes to America as a "beaten and finished man."[30] In America, he finds much suffocation in life and writes in the aforesaid letter, "This is America and we out-produce, out-sell, out-manufacture, out-fight, and out-screw the rest of the world but the latter is elusive."[31]

Like *The Ginger Man*, *A Singular Man* is also a powerful diatribe against the evils of distorted values in an acquisitive society. George Smith, the protagonist of this novel, is a further development of Sebastian Dangerfield. He leads a life of loneliness in spite of huge wealth in his possession. His meetings with others are merely "accidental encounters"[32] for him the world is a world of dazzling wealth which makes Miss Martin, his secretary, feel that "the whole world is horrible and mean."[33] In the midst of the glamour of wealth, Martin feels that wife and children of Smith are alienated: the long hall and staircase are "anonymous." Donleavy introduces an episode in which Smith stands outside his house in the freezing snow calling his sons and daughters to open the door but no one comes. Clarisa, his only daughter, refuses to open the door and says that she does not like him: to his great horror, she says that it is not his house, she says: "We live in it and that means we own it and that means I can keep this door shut and you out of here if I want. I guess you understand English, don't you."[34] George, standing in the freezing snow at the doorstep of his house, muses over his predicament: "if you don't live with kids they grow to hate you. If you live with them they hate you more. Not a shred of respect. Left standing on what technically is my own doorstep."[35] Shirl, his wife, unbolts the door. The dialogue between the husband and wife suggests how George feels himself imprisoned in his own house: "Forgive the chaos, Roger and Wilbur were building a jail on the stairs last night," says Shirl. "For me I suppose,"[36] replies George. Like the earlier hero, George also unsuccessfully searches for love because his first love, whom he later on marries, crushes his craving for genuine affection by her wayward habits and drives him to undertake various sexual adventures with the result that he is isolated from his wife and children and becomes a lonely figure, "a singular man."[37] In this way, Donleavy condemns and protests against the capitalist ethos of naked individualism which destroys the pious values of love.

In the collection of short stories, *Meet My Maker the Mad Molecule*, Donleavy condemns moral perversion as the foremost trait of acquisitiveness and emphasizes the importance of elemental values such as love. The protagonist of his short stories know it very well that it is "anarchy to fly my own personal flag"[38] in ("At Longitude and Latitude"), yet their counterparts in his novels rot in the hell of their own self-indulgent life.

Samuel S (*The Saddest Summer of Samuel S*), who is "one of the points of interest in Europe", is the symbol of European despair.[39] Having led a life of whoring and drinking, he now is overpowered by an urge of procreation and dreams of marrying a girl and having kids but ironically he never talks of love. A woman with a biblical name, Abigail comes in his life who wants to cohabit with him and satisfy her lust but she refuses to marry him. She says that she has "I come all the way to Europe to really get laid", when Samuel says "came all the way to Europe to get really Cured."[40] She explains her notion about man-woman relationship in terms of physical. "My interest is highly scientific biological." Abigail thus appears as a spokesman of free sex of the Beats whom Donleavy is categorically denouncing. At the end of the novella, Samuel wishes to have seen off the woman and her colleague. A fine illustration of the human love kindled in the heart of a bohemian-turn-lover.

The evils of untrammelled passions are condemned in *The Beastly Beatitudes of Balthazar B*. Indulgence in sex and wine is a routine affair in the life of Balthazar and Beefy, "the world's most beatific sinner as the Newsweek called him. Wealth is no problem for them; Balthazar squanders his father's money for enjoying the illusory bliss of life, but the more he tries to 'purchase', happiness, the farther he retreats back into the world of his 'lonely elegance', 'where no one will ever again get to know me'."[41] The illusory freedom of the Black Humorists and the Beatniks is mocked at in the following utterances of Balthazar: "Chains winding round one with an eternal clank. Can't leap from the crapper here and go chasing so hopelessly after freedom. Only thing left now is to rest and ruminate without rusting."[42] Being fed up with the ways of "free" life he has been experimenting, he is tortured by the awareness of his lonely self devoid of love: "One is all alone when you stop somewhere in your life and look at the love spilled from your hands." And ultimately he cries in anguish:

O, my God. How can one ever be. Ideally suited for the whole world. And

A
Popular
Personality.[43]

The character of Beefy is a fine example of the technique of self-mockery and irony which reflects Donleavy's rejection of acquisitiveness suggested by Beefy's sexomania. A few sentences uttered by him will explain the point. "I love sin. That's what I most desire", "I must not be distracted from my mission," "sinful desire consumes me." He drags Balthazar into the sin. He is proud of his lasciviousness: "I think cannibalism is next on my calendar of lusts,"[44] he says to Balthazar. Balthazar is horrified to watch this show of moral debauchery, Beefy's sexual encounters with Breda and Rebecca. Donleavy directly comments on this dreadful drama of moral debauchery: "A college awake this night. For an awarding of a degree. In harlotry."[45] However, he occasionally makes direct statements on the condition of human life. About the life in Dubin, he says, "This city is a sewer flowing with rancor and decomposed "flesh, rotting through all these streets. Disease eats out these hearts. Bodies full of poison." On another occasion, he remarks on the law of the Jungle in morals, "There are no rules down here on the Quay."

Donleavy in the beginning (*The Onion Eaters*) tells about the hero's inheriting the Charnel Castle from his great grand aunt: Clayton Claw Cleaver Clementine who has descended "directly in the main line from Clementine of The Three Glands."[46]

After convalescing in a hospital, Clayton takes the charge of the Castle which is looked after by five unpaid servants. A band of four rogues drops in, uninvited, who pose themselves as scientists but their interest is more in extra academic pursuits, which shows that they are the extension of wild bohemians, as Erconwald makes a confession. "My log book records,...of human sexual unions. Thirteen. Twelve with harlots. Of bestial cohabitations there have been five. I fail to have erection with women to whom I have paid court."[47] Thus, the Charnel Castle becomes the microcosm of the macrocosmic bohemian west.

Clayton, at the end, is left physically exhausted and spiritually broken, he walks alone with his dog, Elmer, and reaches the bank of a brook. Standing there alone, he broods over the modern culture and civilization and sheds tears over the decadent generation of men and women ruining their life today. "Out there far away the rest of the world has gone modern with whole new jumping generations. And holy hell is the only thing we have up-to-date here."[48]

And finally Donleavy's *A Fairy Tale of New York* is an incisive attack upon the American dream of success which has monetized human relation and crushed finer sensibilities. Cornelius Treacle Christian, the protagonist who is left an orphan in early childhood, undertakes the job of a mortician at a funeral parlour in New York out of poverty where he has a series of encounters with a number of girls with whom he does not hesitate to play a nasty game of sexuality and for want of true love is left lonely. The city of New York looks as a "monkey city where everyone is making faces."[49]

Being riven by the horror of loneliness and desolation, he decides to leave New York. His ship pulls out midstream and whistles. Bidding good bye to his native city, he says to himself "You're leaving nowhere when the whole place belongs to someone else.... Travelling east with me out of this city of gloomy coincidence."[50] The ship gathers speed and he imagines that the day is "darkening like the dying." He leans down his head to rest on his hands and feels as if someone were asking him, "Why are you standing. With your hope and sorrows old."[51] He remembers that when he was a little boy one day he went out playing and got lost and told young kids "a fairy tale of New York" that his father was "a tycoon" and his mother "a princess."[52] It was actually a day dreaming on his part to become a rich man, though he was an orphan living at the mercy of a foster mother. In other words, he has been cherishing since his childhood the vision of the American dream of success which shattered into pieces when he confronted the naked realities of life in America and his bohemian desire to enjoy the bliss of wealth and women led him to frustration and loneliness. Thus, this novel presents

Donleavy's strongest protest against valuelessness in American society.

Notes

1. Quoted in "What They Did in Dublin" with *The Ginger Man*, a play in *The Plays of J.P. Donleavy*, Penguin Books Ltd., 1974, p. 38.
2. David Mc Reynolds, "Hipsters Unleashed", Seymour Krim (ed.), *The Beats*, Greenwich: Fawcett Publications, Inc., 1960, pp. 203-04.
3. *Ibid.*, p. 205.
4. *Ibid.*, pp. 205-06.
5. John Clellon Holmes "The Philosophy of The Beat Generation", Semour Krim (ed.), *The Beats*, *op. cit.*, p. 17.
6. *Ibid.*, p. 18.
7. *Ibid.*, p. 22.
8. *Ibid.*, p. 23.
9. Herbert Gold, "The Beat Mystique", Thomas Parkinson (ed.), *A Casebook on the Beats*, New York: Thomas Y. Crowell Company, 1968, p. 250.
10. "The Philosophy of The Beat Generation", *op. cit.*, p. 18.
11. Quoted in *The Beats*, Semour Krim, *op. cit.*
12. Norman Mailer, *The Presidential Papers*, Harmondsworth, Middlesex, Penguin Books Ltd., 1968, p. 200.
13. *Ibid.*, p. 223.
14. *Advertisement for Myself*, London: Panther Books Ltd., 1968, p. 271.
15. *Ibid.*, p. 275.
16. *Ibid.*, p. 279.
17. *The Presidential Papers*, *op. cit.*, p. 266.
18. *The Advertisement for Myself*, *op. cit.*, p. 285.
19. *The Presidential Papers*, *op. cit.*, p. 271.
20. *The Advertisement for Myself*, *op. cit.*, p. 285.
21. *Ibid.*, p. 286.
22. *Idem.*
23. "The Philosophy of The Beat Generation", p. 14.
24. Carolyn Gaiser, "Georgory Corso: A Poet, the Beatway" in *A Casebook on the Beats*, (ed.) Thomas Parkinson, *op. cit.*, p. 270.

25. Bernard Duffey, "The Three Works of Jack Kerouac", Joseph J. Waldmeir (ed.), *Recent American Fiction: Some Critical Views*, Boston: Houghton Miffin Company, 1963, p. 175.
26. J.P. Donleavy, *The Ginger Man*, Harmondsworth Middlesex, England: Penguin Books Ltd., 1955, p. 93.
27. *Ibid.*, p. 26.
28. Jerry H. Bryant, *The Open Decision: The Contemporary American Novel and Its Intellectual Background*, New York: The Free Press, London: Collier Macmillan, 1970, p. 210.
29. *The Ginger Man*, pp. 81-82.
30. *Ibid.*, p. 238.
31. *Ibid.*, pp. 332-33.
32. J.P. Donleavy, *A Singular Man*, Harmondsworth, Middlesex, Penguin Books Ltd., 1963, p. 5.
33. *Ibid.*, p. 49.
34. *Ibid.*, p. 64.
35. *Idem.*
36. *Ibid.*, p. 65.
37. *Ibid.*, p. 49.
38. "At Longitude and Latitude", p. 28.
39. J.P. Donleavy, *The Saddest Summer of Samuel S*, Harmondsworth, Middlesex, Penguin Books Ltd., 1968, p. 30.
40. *Ibid.*, p. 95.
41. *Idem.*
42. J.P. Donleavy, *The Beastly Beatitudes of Balthazar B*, Harmondsworth, Middlesex, Penguin Books Ltd., p. 322.
43. *Ibid.*, p. 326.
44. *Ibid.*, p. 212.
45. *Ibid.*, p. 213.
46. J.P. Donleavy, *The Onion Eaters*, Harmondsworth, Middlesex, London: Penguin Books Ltd., 1971, p. 6.
47. *Ibid.*, p. 37.
48. *Ibid.*, p. 289.
49. J.P. Donleavy, *A Fairy Tale of New York*, Harmondsworth Middlesex, London: Penguin Books Ltd., 1973, p. 312.
50. *Ibid.*, p. 333.
51. *Idem.*
52. *Ibid.*, p. 334.

Chapter 14

Humanism in John Steinbeck's *The Grapes of Wrath*

The paper is a modest attempt to understand in what measure the philosophical formulations of humanism have gone in shaping the novel's thesis, which is partly derived from the value, associated with the Jaffersonian Agrarian society the ideal of which lost its appeal with the disappearance of the family-size farm from the American scene after the great war, the Transcendental optimism and the Protestant doctrine of self-reliance, especially of Emerson and Thoreau, and from Whitman's idea of mass democracy and respect for manual labour. Malcolm Bradbury talks of the 'biological evolutionism', expressing Steinbeck's theories of instinctive collective existence, which is beautifully reflected in the 'parable of the tortoise which is the oldest form of animal life', symbolizing people and their struggle. What really seems to matter the story purports to convey, is not whether people reach the destination or not, what is significant is the action which is paramount to create illusion of living in the midst of an absurd icy desert: the indomitable striving of the tortoise, as if driven by a superior power and the survival of those migrants who reached California in face of the terror of history, throws over the novel a gloss of allegory, transcending place and time.

However, let us be precise about what the term "humanism" implies and how it becomes manifest in the novel which is read as a novel of social protest by virtue of its use of great Depression as a backdrop. In post-war period, the American capitalism and industrialism became triumphant: the machines uprooted men from their lands, with which they had deep-seated ties of belongingness. Hence, the parting is painful that we see in the protest of the Grampa, which is, though ineffectual, being a case of tragic irony. Pa Joad feels surprised to see him unwilling to be bundled up with the family.

> "Not goin?" Pa demanded. "What you mean you ain't a-goin? Why, here we're all packed up, ready. We got to go. We got no place to stay."
>
> "I ain't sayin' for you to stay," said Grampa. "You go right on along. Me—I'm stayin'. I give her a goin'—over all night mos'ly. This here's my country. I b'long here. An' I don't give a goddamn if they's oranges an' grapes crowdin' a fella outa bed even. I ain't a-goin'. This country ain't no good, but it's my country. No, you all go ahead. I'll jus' stay right here where I b'long."[1]

Attempts have been made from the beginning to fit the term 'humanism' into the framework of theology, philosophy, history, each study has a print of bias which has made the task to find out a viable definition of the word rather arduous whether the term is a religious doctrine, a scientific theory, or a term of ethics.

The term 'humanism' comes from the Latin word 'humanista', which in English means 'humanist'. A humanist was a professor, a student of a well-defined cycle of subjects, known as the *studia humanitatis*, which includes the study of grammar, rhetoric, history, poetry and moral philosophy. The period of early Renaissance was called by the name of humanism which was the period of intellectual preparation, a period in which the Greek and Latin texts were introduced into the university curriculum and bring by way of translations, the wisdom of the ancients, contained therein, within the reach of the common man. It was designated as classical humanism which was characterized by scholarship and learning. Even to quote a single line from the Greek and Latin authors was a mark of classical humanism. But the term tended to be disputable with the rise of modern notion of humanism, when several schools of humanism of disparate shades sprang up, such as the theistic/atheistic humanism, scientific humanism, christian humanism and the like. Paul Oskar

Kristeller, the prime authority on the Renaissance humanism, says that it is the result of a tendency growing up today that if humanism is to be made acceptable to contemporary opinion, it must be defined in terms of certain ideas and ideals, which is perhaps due to "the declining respect for scholarship."[2]

The classical humanism has been associated with the Renaissance and its classical studies for more than a hundred years, but in recent times it has become a subject of philosophical and historical confusion. Any one, showing a kind of concern with human values today is called a humanist to the effect that the term 'humanism' has became a rather "elusive label of praise", whereas in the Renaissance, it had a different meaning: a student of *studia-humanitatis* was called a humanist. Kristeller says that what he understands by the term 'humanism' is that it is "a body of literature, scholarship and thought, represented by the writing of the humanists", and the humanists are "those scholars who by profession or vocation were concerned with the *studia humanitatis*"[3] and thus if there exists any confusion it is because of one reason that the manner in which humanism is defined, tells more about the definer's ideological convictions, rather than the term itself, and partly by man's misunderstanding of it, after his elevation in the scheme of things, as the centre of the universe, even by the time of the early Florentine Platonists, like Ficino, his disciple Pico Mirandolla and Pomponazzi. This brought a shift from theocentrism to anthropocentrism, thereby taking man away from his divine source and leaving him thus spiritually impoverished. It is partly by how Maritain[4] defines humanism and Bedyaev's discovery of the self-destructive tendencies with humanism[5] that it is both attacked and defended. Notwithstanding, the gains of humanism were misconstrued by those who were the victims of glorification of self and looked the world, not on God's term, but on their own.

Paul Kurtz writes that the 20th century has been proclaimed as the Humanist century in the sense that here the anti-humanist illusions, inherited from the previous ages, are seriously questioned and shattered. Which is why we hear terms like the scientific humanism, the heretical humanism, the anthropocentric humanism. Miriam Allen deFord says "Humanism in my viewpoint must be atheistic or it is not humanism as I understand."[6] But it is not that man is not aware of the moral significance of the two principles of humanism which are freedom and responsibility: freedom, he understands, is not laisez-faire in morals and thus he feels himself largely responsible for his own destiny. He knows that there are no saints or utopias and the salvation does not lie outside his own control. The humanist alternative in this respect offers man a realistic appraisal of the human condition and the promise of ameliorating it. But it does not mean the anarchic affirmation of self, he knows that the value lies in what we try and what happens to us in the striving. This is the humanism of the Joads, who believe in the human potentialities and striving and do not deny the Transcendental God.

This school of humanism is reflected in the structural design, language and characterization. Characters are invested with a vision which is, through and through, humanistic in principle and action. They exit in the story, primarily by means of practicing a humanity-centred philosophy, which does not remove them from the framework of orthodox christianity, for the fact that the religion they believe in is a new religion which is a variant of A. Comte's "religion of humanity". If Casy withdraws from preaching, finding the dogma inadequate to resolve human problems, it is not atheism, rather it is illumination to interpret christianity as he understands it. His concern for humanity is reflected in the belief that

> moral values must be removed from the mantle of theological dogma, and a conviction that our moral ideas must be constantly re-examined and revised in the light of the present needs and social demands.[7]

Steinbeck exploits their belief that human nature is essentially good in creating a meaning in the role the characters play in the novel. We read how the Joad family, on way to California, the biblical Promised Land of plenty milk and honey, sustain their courage and moral fibre, being influenced by Casy's sermonizing about the inseparable ties between the Holy Spirit and the human spirit, the soul of each individual being one small part of the Big Soul, Tom voices the same faith in the transcendental optimism at the time of departure at the end, while comforting his mother that it really does not matter whether he lives or dies, he would be near to them in time of trouble.

Ma Joad also has faith in this doctrine which is reflected in her counseling Tom when he talks of violence which is contrary to the norm of human decency and the faith in progress.

> "Easy," she said. "You got to have patience. Why, Tom—us people will go on livin' when all them people is gone. Why, Tom, we're the people that live. They ain't goona wipe us out. Why, we're the people—we go on."[8]

Jim Casy is introduced as an ex-preacher. Once he was "Reverend Jim Casy", but now just 'Casy' getting "the call no more. Got a lot of sinful ideas, but they seem kinda sensible"[9] He is the central figure to live by Steinbeck's theories of collective existence and promote the same in others by means of philosophizing. He is admitted to the Joad fold in Ch. 10 by Ma's 'A-men', when he comes to seek permission if he could go west with them. He tells why he has given up baptizing and preaching, finding it barren and abstract.

> "I ain't gonna baptize. I'm gonna work in the fiel's, in the green fiel's, an' I'm gonna be near to folks. I ain't gonna try to teach 'em nothin'. I'm gonna try to learn. Gonna learn why the folks walks in the grass, gonna hear 'em talk, gonna hear 'em sing. Gonna listen to kids eatin' sauce. Gonna her husban' an' wife a-poudin' the mattress in the night. Gonna eat with 'em an' learn." His eyes were wet and shining, "gonna lay 'in the grass, open an' honest with anybody that'll have me. Gonna cuss an' swear an' hear the poetry of folks talkin'. All that's holy, all that's what I didn' understan'. All them things is the good things."[10]

Why does he feel so despaired and disillusioned by the religious beliefs and choose to live in the midst of the common folks to have a feel of reality?

Broadly speaking, Humanism, the dictionary defines, is a system of thought that considers that it is important to solve human problems by reason than by religious beliefs, which is why he rejects congregation and cannot support the idea of sin and salvation, as the scriptures say, he also grows skeptical about the spiritual efficacy of the prayer. But it is not that he has turned atheistic, or that his humanism is anthropocentric humanism. In the Neoplatonist tradition, the excellence and human dignity is emphasized because of immortality of soul. Casy is moved by this idea of human spirit and it is in the sense that his humanism can also be interpreted as the humanism of the Greeks which is christian humanism, which tells that "one can be pro-man without being anti-God." His faith in the progress finds expression in a fine speech, when he is asked by Joad to explain, "What did you figger?"

> I figgered about the Holy Sperit and the Jesus road. I figgered, 'Why do we got to hang it on God or Jesus? Maybe,' I figgered, 'maybe it's all men an' all women we love; maybe that's the Holy Sperit—the human sperit—the whole shebang. Maybe all men got one big soul ever'body's a part of.' Now I sat there thinkin' it, an' all of a suddent—I knew it. I knew it so deep down that it was true, and I still know it.[11]

Steinbeck introduces an encounter in Ch. 26 in which both Tom and Casy are pursued by the deputies who try to escape but are overpowered. Casy makes a humanistic appeal to stir their conscience which raises him to Christ-figure.

> A sharp call. "There they are!" Two flashlight beams fell on the men, caught them, blinded them. "Stand where you are." The voices came out of the darkness. "That's him. That shiny bastard. That's him."
>
> Casy stared blindly at the light. He breathed heavily. "Listen," he said. "You fellas don' know what you're doin'. You're helpin' to starve kids."
>
> "Shut up, you red son-of-a-bitch."
>
> A short heavy man stepped into the light. He carried a new white pick handle.
>
> Casy went on, "You don' know what you're a-doin."[12]

The tormentors really do not know what they are doing, they do not know that they themselves are as much victim of the system as the migrant farmers, called the Okies, they were persecuting. Casy is killed and Tom in retaliation kills a deputy but is injured in the fight. He goes in hiding to escape arrest. Tom's protection is an ordeal but it is the woman who shows more resourcefulness and insight than man to surmount the crisis. Ma replaces Pa as authority to protect Tom. She says, "Pa has lost his place. He ain't the head no more. We're cracking up, Tom there ain't no fambly now."[13]

Tom Joad is introduced as a slowly-awakening disciple of Casy, who further takes up his mission after his martyrdom. Tom's humanism is theistic humanism which recognizes that the centre for man is God. His moral transformation from an individualist to a man of social concern owes to Casy's philosophizing of the purity and the transcending power of human spirit. He has learnt by experience that what is important is action, in terms of the whole, than the particular individual. It is by means of collective organized labour and protest that they can face the heat of the economic squeeze. It so happens that Ruthie, in frenzy of childish humour, tells the agents about Tom's hiding which makes things ugly for the mother to manage. To Ma's question "How am I gonna a know about you? They might kill ya am I n't know," what Tom says is a final acceptance of Casy's gospel of the social action. He says that he will be around everywhere which is what Casy said "a man does not have a soul of his own but only a small piece of big soul, the Over soul."

Tom brushes aside Ma's fears laughingly but underneath there lurks the darkening shadows of the impending tragedy.

> Tom laughed uneasily, "Well, maybe like Casy says, a fella ain't got a soul of his own, but on'y a piece of a big one-an' then—"
>
> "Then what, Tom?"
>
> "Then it don' matter. Then I'll be all aroun' in the dark. I'll be ever'where—wherever you look. Wherever they's a fight so hungry people can eat. I'll be there. Wherever they's a cop beatin'up a guy, I'll be there. If Casy knowed, why, I'll be in the way guys yell when they're mad an'-I'll be in the way kids laugh when they're hungry an'

> they know supper's ready. An' when our folks eat the stuff they raise an' live in the houses they build—why, I'll be there. See? God, I'm talkin' like Casy. Comes of thinkin' about him so much. Seems like I can see him sometimes."[14]

The women characters too are Steinbeck's class illustration and exemplification in humanism, they are humanistic to the core which is manifest in their attitude towards self and society. The tenants are the victims of the socio-economic determinism, beyond their control and understanding but it is the women who face the crisis in a more humanely and pragmatic fashion.

Ma Joad is drawn as a Promethean figure, representing the turtle's stubborn determination to somehow keep living. As a humanist, she is moved by Casy's philosophies of transcendental faith which is reflected, not only in how she holds together the Joad family from falling apart but in how she comforts the fellow migrants, the Wilsons and shares food with the starving Hooverville children. It reaches the acme at the end in Ch. 30 wherein Steinbeck creates a situation to test one's gold of humanity. She urges upon her daughter, Rose of Sharon to save a dying old man by starving in the barn by means of breast feeding. It is a rare example which is hard to be seen in an uprooted segment of humanity.

The episode in which Ma is helped by a poor storekeeper is a fine illustration of humanism as a human programme. It so happens that Ma goes to a store to buy the needful grocery items from a Hooper ranch, the only dollar, she has is consumed in the melee of the exorbitant prices and she has, nothing extra to buy sugar. Seeing the woman in trouble, the storekeeper who is mortally afraid of the owner, gives her a loan of ten cents from his own pocket to enable her buy sugar for the family. It is a rare gesture of selfless service to suffering humanity in hard times which reminds us of a Dickens's central character, a Betsy Trotwood or a Brownlow who act as Christ figure for the orphan.

What Ma has learnt during the process that it is the poor who can help a poor in time of need, goes like a gospel of poverty divinized. It is unnecessary to ask whether the voice is of hers or of the novelist, what she says is a fine reflection of the attitude of the bourgeois and the proletarian towards human suffering.

> If you're in trouble, or hurt or need—go to the poor people.
> They're the only ones, that will help you—the only ones.[15]

Ma's humanitarian world outlook and her faith in the principle of existence and continuity of life is further shared by her eldest daughter, Rose of Sharon. She is drawn, next to Casy as a Christ-figure. She is married and is in the advanced stage of pregnancy. She has faith in the doctrine of biological evolutionism which is manifest in the last chapter in which she gives breast-feeding to an old starving man after the delivery of a still born child. Ma takes out the old man's boy and her another child daughter, Ruthie, leaving Rose of, Sharon, sitting still in the whispering barn. The moment in crucial for people to redefine themselves.

The novelist tells

> She moved slowly to the corner and stood looking down at the wasted face, into the wise, frightened eyes. Then slowly she lay down beside him. He shook his head slowly from side to side. Rose of Sharon loosened one side of the blanket and bared her breast. "You got to," she said. She squirmed closer and pulled his head close. "There!" she said, "There," her hand moved behind his head and supported it. Her fingers moved gently in his hair. She looked up and across the barn, and her lips came together and smiled mysteriously.[16]

Some find the ending disturbing that it is tendentiousness and a show of sentimentalism which is not fair. Steinbeck uses the instinct of survival as a powerful symbol of life to go on living somehow in face of the threats of the forces, both human and natural.

It is Rose of Sharon's humanism, and her faith in the pantheistic doctrine of Oneness of all which transcends her tragedy, knowing no barriers. What she does is the apparent expression of Casy's philosophizing which Ma has also voiced twice in the novel, "We'll do what we got to do," and "use to be the family was faust. It's not now. It's anybody. Worse off we get, the more we got to do."[17]

Thus, despite the serious criticism,[18] the novel, since its appearance (1939) has not been out of print, the reason of its population is rooted partly in Ma's prophetic proclamations which are humanistic in conception and a corollary of what J.P. Van Praag says, while defining humanism.

> Humanism attempts to provide a coherent answer to the question of human existence and assumes that existence can be made worthwhile by the realization of everyone's possibilities in devotion to a common humanity.[19]

Notes

1. John Steinbeck, *The Grapes of Wrath*, Penguin Books Ltd., 1967, p. 114.
2. Paul Oskar Kristeller, *Renaissance Thought: Papers on Humanism and the Arts*, New York: Harper and Row Publishers, 1965, p. 54.
3. *Ibid.*, p. 70.
4. "The first kind of humanism recognizes that the centre for man is God, it implies the christian conception of man as at once a sinner and redeemed, and the christian conception of grace and freedom.... The second kind of humanism beehives that man is his own centre, and therefore the centre of all things. It implies a naturalistic conception of man and of freedom."

   Quoted in M.M. Mahood, *Poetry and Humanism*, London: The Comlet Press Ltd., 1958, p. 12.
5. "Humanism, as its name implies, denotes the elevation and setting up of man in the centre of the universe.... It has been said that humanism discovered the human individuality and gave it full play, freeing it from its medieval subjection and directing it upon free paths of self-affirmation and creation. But humanism also contained a diametrically opposite principle, that of man's abasement, of the exhaustion of his creative powers and of his general enfeeblement.... In fact, humanism denied that man was the image and likeness of God; that he was the reflection of the Divine Being.... The christian consciousness of man began to lose its strength. And this, in its turn, gave rise to a self-destructive dialectic within humanism."

   Ibid., p. 13.

6. "Heretical Humanism", Paul Kurtz, ed., *The Humanist Alternative: Some Definitions of Humanism*, London: Pemberton Books, 1973, p. 77.
7. Paul Kurtz, "Humanism and the Moral Revolution", in *The Humanist Alternative: Some Definitions of Humanism*, *op. cit.*, p. 49.
8. *The Grapes of Wrath*, p. 293.
9. *Ibid.*, p. 22.
10. *Ibid.*, p. 98.
11. *Ibid.*, p. 26.
12. *Ibid.*, p. 404.
13. *Ibid.*, p. 411.
14. *Ibid.*, p. 39.
15. *Ibid.*, p. 326.
16. *Ibid.*, p. 476.
17. *Ibid.*, p. 465.
18. The publication of the novel (1939) which won the Pulitzer Prize, created a stir: the charges of serious nature were laid against it which speaks of a subjective bias, such as that it is "a lie, a black infernal creation of a twisted distorted mind, a propaganda of communist ideology". Frederick I. Carpenter reads it as a novel of "American dream", to Joseph W. Beach it is one of the finest American novels. It is read as a novel of social despair, than a piece of fiction and Steinbeck is accused of being a revolutionary, whereas the truth is, as W. French argues, that he is a reformer, not a revolutionary, his call is both to the working class and the economic barons to change their attitude towards each other. "His condemnation of the evils of naked individualism and the vulgar hedonistic acquisitiveness becomes powerfully manifest in his own words, 'The quality of owning freezes you forever into 'I' and cut you off ever from the 'We'.'" Its popularity can be judged by the fact that the film made on it stays as the best of the era.
19. "What is Humanism", in the *Humanist Alternative: Some Definitions of Humanism*, p. 45.

Chapter 15

Saul Bellow's *The Dean's December*: 'Self as rebel'

The various dimensions, Bellow—criticism hinges on, are the novelist's ideological convictions, the nature and problem of self in relation to the philosophy of rebellion, Camus puts forth in. *The Rebel*, and the discovery of reality, which Ihab Hassan says "now-a-days borrows the disguises of chaos." Bellow's own remark is worth quoting, "People do not appear to respond as they once did to the various faces of reality. Innumerable things intervene to cloud or modify relations."[1] Yet it is not all.

Another crucial question, haunting Bellow's imagination from the start is the quality of living—how a good man should live—which is all pervasive in his writings, right from his first novel, *Dangling Man* (1944) to *The Dean's December* (1982) Joseph's primary concern, as we see, is to discover how to be good. He is aware of the ironies of existence in a milieu which is not wholesome to the growth of human values and therefore to live as good man involves suffering and alienation. He dismisses alienation as "a fool's plea.... And was I to become this whole man alone, without aid?"[2] In other words, he has learnt by experience that it is by being in the world that one can be fully himself, which is a concept of participation and involvement, being illustrated in Sartrean third dimension of Being—'Being-with-Others'.

Bellow is an existential humanist. He has faith in human potential and human striving, since impassiveness generates nihilism and moral confusion. He draws on Sartrean view of man as 'project' who, to begin with, is nothing, and becomes at the end what he makes of himself. "Existentionalism never takes man as the end, since man is still to be determined."[3] Satire takes Dostoevsky remark: "If God did not exist, everything would be permitted," as the starting point of existentialism and later writes that the real problem is not whether God does/does not exist, but the discovery of self, and the need to understand that man alone is the "legislator" and, therefore, it is not by turning back upon himself but always by seeking beyond himself that "he can realize himself as truly human."

Second, Bellow's view of reality is shaped by Camusian concept of a rebel protagonist whose passion is to live life as it comes to live by. A Bellow protagonist acts as rebel, not to reject the system but to come to terms to reality as it exists, since the point is to live. It is in this sense that all his protagonists are positive creations who push the rock upward to the top to seek fulfillment, taking it as fate, as Sisyphus does, believing in human striving that "There is no fate that cannot be surmounted by scorn."[4] Rebellion, Camus says, is one of man's essential dimensions the historic reality of which cannot be denied. The rebel is a humanist to the core, if humanism offers a realistic appraisal of the human condition and the promise of ameliorating it, the rebel defies, more than he denies. "Rebellion is the common ground on which every man bases his first values. I rebel, therefore, we exist."[5]

The fact is illustrated by what happen to the protagonist, Albert Corde, who happens to be the Dean of Colleges in the University of Chicago, and his Rumanian wife who is an astronomer. They go to Bucharest to attend on his ailing mother-in-law, Valeria, who is kept in a Party hospital which she herself had it built when she was the health minister.

The Dean's December is an extension of the themes of Saul Bellow's earlier novels, the one being most crucial that haunted American imagination in the "forties"—'how to be human?' The protagonist's moral awakening to the contemporary reality is rooted in the socio-historical reality—its one fixture of apocalyptic dismay is being represented by Chicago, the native city of Albert Corde, riven by violence and gangsterism, rapes and murder, crimes and moral degeneration against which a struggle is misconstrued as treachery, racism and buffoonery, the other is the oppressive environment of Rumanian metropolis, Bucharest, reeling under the wheel of a totalitarian communist order. In Bucharest, Corde is horrified by the treatment meted out to Valaria, and her daughter, Minna, in Chicago he is persistently haunted by a nightmare which is all a machination of man's is humanity to man. But does he break? No, certainly not. If he resigns from deanship, it is not defeatism or failure, but a human protest against the system which needs a moral purge.

Bellow's vision is essentially that of an accommodationist, his hero comes to accept facts of existence as they are which is a value in the philosophy of rebellion because confrontation is a disvalue, leading one nowhere, and because rebellion is affirmative, Corde evolves his own strategy of survival to seek fulfillment.

The tales of the two cities—Chicago and Bucharest—are fused together to act as a gigantic metaphor of human suffering, as experienced by man under the two sets of value system—communism and capitalism. The Chicagoan universe, which in the words of the novelist is "the contempt centre of the USA"[6] is an enigma for the protagonist to survive for its collapse of moral standards of life, coldness and extinction of what is good and human, as suggested by the word 'December' in the title. December heralds the end of the year but in the two far-flung cities, Bucharest and Chicago, the month signifies more than the ending of the year: it is the culture which is itself dying to be replaced by the machinery of power which is hostile and retrograde to the growth of the finer values of life. The cultural chaos is suggested by the freezing water—whereas the institutionalised life in Bucharest is symbolic of repressions, destructions, blockades and surveillance which man highly resents, but they exist as encroachments to bulldoze human perception.

The novel opens in Bucharest with the comments: "Corde, who led the life of an executive in America—wasn't a college dean, a kind of executive?"[7] which is rather disturbing but revealing the interrogative tone is a clear indication that Corde's deanship has already been in jeopardy? We wonder what it could be, the wrath of the system or a bane of elitist bias? Minna was educated in Rummania, a communist country, and is presently working as a professor of astronomy in Mount Palomar Observatory. She comes back home with her husband after twenty years when her mother is struggling for life. Corde was earlier a journalist but resigned for having "cultural inclinations you couldn't satisfy by journalism"[8] and this brought his transfer from Paris to Chicago.

Corde and Minna are putting up at Valeria's old-fashioned apartment in Bucharest. The novelist introduces the heterogeneous images of the "earthquake-damaged buildings, winter skies, gray pigeons, pollard trees, squalid orange-rusty trams hissing under trolley cables, which are symbolic of the decay and disjunctedness of life pattern in a regimented-power structure society.

Bellow's description of the crowed that gathers at the cemetery to attend Valeria's funeral is a peculiar product of man's show of the fascistic leanings in his conduct. The overwhelming sense of fear, gloom and stiffness suggests that the very spirit of life is hardened, signifying death in life.

> Some of them could not easily raise their heads for identification, their neck muscles had grown so stiff. Yes, many had the cervical arthrosia. There were splashes of dark pigment of their faces. Old mouths gaped up at you when they spoke.... They came...well, they had their reasons. They came also to remind Minna of their existence, 'yes, we're still here, in case you wondered, and we could tell you plenty. And your mother' she got you away, it was one of her great successes. Good for you. And for her. Now it's over for her, and soon for us, too. And this is what turns us out, in this gloom.[9]

A subtle contrast is introduced between the quality of life as lived by the masses under the old regime and the new order. The crowd was like a demonstration that came to pay regards to Valeria and also to see the American couple, Corde and Minna, but the real purpose was, as Valeria's sister, Gigi, explains, to tell "the regime something", which was definitely a reflection and exposure of excesses perpetrated on them by the new communist regime.

> It wasn't because Valeria had fallen from grace, or because she had stood up to the Politburo or the central committee, or refused years later to rejoin the Party when they invited her. They came out with a sort of underfed dignity in what was left of their presocialist wardrobe, to affirm that there was a sort of life—and perhaps, as communists or even Iron Guardists (it was conceivable), they had signed against it—the old European life which at its most disgraceful was infinitely better than this present one.[10]

The predatory nature of the state now, as it was in the past, dots on inconceivable atrocities but the *modus operandi* has changed. It is reported that,

> ...according to Amnesty International they inject mind drugs in psychiatric hospitals, and who knows how many people are dying in those places. Electric shocks, sulfadiazine injection. And it was much rawer before when the Colonel was an apprentice. One of my mother-in-law's colleagues, an apprentice. One of Justice, has his head hacked off in his cell. They decided not to bring him to trial.[11]

After Valeria's death Minna, feels unsafe with Corde, who is a foreigner in Bucharest in her own home country. She fears any moment an assault of the power centre on their humanity, which is why she does not let Corde out alone, thinking that they might pick him up on some pretext, and "that would really complicate things."

And what they apprehend becomes a reality. Corde confronts the real horror of this 'socialist paradise' when the question of Valeria's funeral arrangement comes up and the decision of the 'higher ups' is more a show of their callousness and petty class prejudices which, as moral decency demands, ought to have been shed with the dead. They go beyond the grave which is a sure symptom of the system reaching putrescence. They were hard on Valeria saying that her daughter sought defection from the Party, whereas the fact was that she protected Minna from the vengeance of the power hierarchy of the police state and endured ostracism while fighting the officials. She finally got "her daughter out of the country." The rigidity and the bureaucratic stiffness of the power machinery becomes manifest in the Colonel's behaviour in the hospital who is a by-product of the system: he got training in psychiatric institutions to crush the dissidents like mentally degenerated persons. But thoughts, as such, have little impact on Corde's consciousness. The sense of mortality and its encounter at the crematorium teaches him how life is to be accepted in its wholeness, the essence of which lies in developing a sense of fellow feelings and universal brotherhood:

> He was not entirely himself—the inward fever, ice in the system, he felt disarticulated. But why should he expect to be himself? At the crematorium he had gone through a death rehearsal. You couldn't rehearse death gratis: It has to cost something.[12]

Corde is well conversant with the brutal realities of life confronting man under a totalitarian value structure in a world which is governed by the tactics to bedevil and denaturalise man, he is driven to a situation of utter helplessness and desolation. The novelist's dig at one anti-human and nightmarish feature of communist order is reflected in setting a pain-level for the people and the irony is that they rationalized the harshness of this schematization by calling it a liberal socialist phase of political philosophy which borders on the senselessness of violence, regimentation and repression of human interest.

Chicago is another universe with a different power structure, Corde is attached to by strong feelings since it is the city of his childhood. What happens there is all a dismal story. It so happens that a white student, Richie Lester, is murdered by the two blacks, Lucas Ebry and his accomplice, a black whore, Riggie Hines, for which Corde as a dean held himself morally responsible. He got involved in the matter to get the whole case thoroughly investigated and brought the criminals to conviction. And because he is a highly delicate and sensitive person, he could not reconcile with the all-pervasive sense of physical and human destruction in the city. Sensing that there is some wrong somewhere, the self rises in rebellion, Corde writes two disturbingly mystifying articles about the moral and cultural climate, pervading the city in the Harper's, that evidently nettled the college authorities. It created a stir, whereas the truth is that the articles make no assault on any one's humanity, rather it is reality and realism which must stay.

The manner in which the college office is stuffed with complaints and objections, as if those Harper pieces had stirred a hornet's nest, is a reflection of the fact how the moral aspect of American reality is outraged. A militant group, known as the Revolutionary Marxist, declare Corde a racist and pass a resolution that he should seek a public apology to the blacks for presenting them as animals and savages. Some were critical of Corde, having no sense of history. They said,

> "The author is a Brahmin. The Brahmins taught us to despise the cities, which accordingly became despicable." Mr. Corde believes in gemulichkeit more than in public welfare. And what makes him think that what it takes to save little black kids is to get them to read Shakespeare? Next he will suggest that we teach them Demonsthenes and make speeches in Greek. The answer to juvenile crime is not in *King Lear* or *Macbeth*.[13]

The charge of racism is something which is unpalatable and morally offensive but it is less damaging to Corde than to the revelers who play a partisan role which is a reflection of their shallow world outlook. Alec Witt, the Provost, gets very angry with the Dean, whose moral duty, he thinks, was to protect the dignity of the office of the deanship. The truth is that he has personal dislike for Corde. Corde was a "high principled idiot dean" in his view and thus his appointment has been a mistake." He takes upon himself the responsibility to "clear up the mess." For the Provost, Corde

> ...was an outsider, he hadn't come up from the academic ranks, hadn't been shaped by the Ph.D. process. It wasn't even clear why he had wanted to become an academic, and even an administrator.[14]

Alec is a prototype of the Colonel in Bucharest—he represents power "qualified by the higher deviousness as power usually was" and Corde's mistake was that he challenged this 'real world of power.' The college wanted Corde to get a clearance for the publication of the articles. The novelist employs the device of irony to debunk Alec's magnanimity that even on the day of Valeria's death when Corde needs peace, the Provost indulges in pestering-campaign by connecting himself with the dean on the telephone.

> The Provost said, "You may not have heard that you were subpoenaed by your cousin."
>
> "Is that so?"
>
> "Mr. Detillion wanted to put you on the stand to establish the heavy involvement of the college in this case. I've checked into that with our legal department...".
>
> "With some real lawyers...."[15]

Corde is also accused of passionately defending the Ridpath who took over as the director of the County Jail. Ridpath was locked into mortal battle to flush out crime and corruption from the jail which was run by the criminals. Corde's defence of Ridpath speaks of his sense of humanity and concern with the predicament of the blacks, being put on the cross. It is in Camusian sense the submission of the individual for the common good. Corde sees in Ridpath the reflection of the old pattern of relationship, existing between the blacks and the whites, which in the present, he finds sadly missing. The dean is wounded in his highest conscience to see the black image destroyed by the black gangs.

Corde's sympathy for the blacks, branded as the underclass by the whites in a parochially narrow moralistic American society, is apparent. "What is with this Professor? What's he talking? His pilot light is gone."[16] And certainly what is tragic is that Corde's moral gesture and attitude to evil cannot have human appreciation in so morally a slippery universe. According to the Dean, "a moral revolution is required." The capitalist class condemns the blacks to unimaginable suffering and death, as if they were not human and were born to writhe like worms crushed under the white boots.

The traditions which segregate the blacks, Corde feels, be demolished and a new value-structure, good and human, be evolved to recognize the human in them in the interest of humanity. This is also a grim reality that their saviours have to bear the brunt of the elite class in that they are side-lined and alienated in the social circle as 'traitor' or a 'fool'. This was one aspect of American reality that Corde attacked in the articles and that evidently unnerved the elitist sensibility.

Further Corde's social concern with the well-being of the community is powerfully reflected in the publication of the discovery of Professor Beech's 'Lead-Poisoning Project.' The scientists have shown the deadening effect of lead on human sensibility which must be checked if humanity is to survive. The idea that lead-contact can destroy the very life-sensitivity fills the mind of the elite class to destroy the initiation in the under classes.

Beech's conclusion of lead-poisoning are undoubtedly deadly and Corde fully stands by him that man be made aware of the risk involved in his constantly being near to it. Its natural corollary is socio-cultural and moral pollution. It permanently effects nervous system, the intellectual faculties are impaired and the kids become "restless, frantic" and develop behaviour-problems. One tragic aspect of Beech's apocalypse is that an escape from the lead contact is impossible:

> So the bottom line is that we eat and drink lead, we breathe it. It accumulates in the seas, which are getting heavier by the day, and it's absorbed by plants and stockpiled in the calcium of the bones. Brains are being mineralized. The great reptiles with their small brains wore thick armor, but our big brains are being hardened from within.[17]

Codre's criticism of the media, the academics who are ruled by public opinion and the universities, has its moral justification as these agencies, being the vital forms of rousing human consciousness have turned passive in the task assigned to them.

Dewey Spengler as a member of the elite class is critical of Corde's moral battling against the collapse of urban America which speaks of his elitist bias. What Dewey is vocal about is the language Corde used in the two articles that it made a mess of his viewpoint which was far from being true; "The Dean's problem had been one of language. Nobody will buy what you're selling—not in those words. They don't even know what your product is."[18]

The problem with Dewey is the spell of socialistic philosophies of Rousseau and the concept of egalitarian societies Corde comes under, for which he gave up the successful career of journalism to be an academician, hoping to fulfill their ideal of creating high human types, the individuals who "would satisfy the human need for stature and love of the beautiful." It is in this context that Corde's resolution to resign from the college job and to go with Minna to Mount Palomar is a fine illustration of the self, gaining a new vision of social concern. He enters the lift following Minna, the lift begins to rise taking Corde higher into another zone of ultimate reality—of the stars and the heaven where the human and the non-human, the finite and the infinite meet.

> The interior was abolished altogether—no interior nothing but the open, freezing heavens. If this present motion were to go on, you would travel straight out. You would go up into the stars.[19]

Some could say that Corde's rejection of the brutal realities of life in Chicago is a gesture of romantic separatism but it is not so. The truth is that he accepts, like Sammler, this universe to be his planet on which he has to live. Up in the air the tension, though a part of cosmic design, leads to harmony and thus the self gains illumination, harmony and poise.

> The sky was tense with stars, but not so tense as he was, in his breast. Everything overhead was in equilibrium, kept in place by mutual tensions. What was it that his tensions kept in place?[20]

The self in the state of moral illumination has the vision of its own reflection into the nature of reality of the material world which, to ordinary eyes, looks like Plato's cave-reality, reflecting shadows within shadows. And his problem is now not how to change the ontological nature of the world, as it stands in all its vileness and sublimity, but to evolve his own pattern of living, keeping in sight to the chaos, as created by the forces of disvalues for want of absolutes in a pluralistic society. And thus Corde, as a seeker after moral truths of life grounded in social realities, survives the nightmare of the Darwanian jungle-morality in Chicago and the repressive, anti-human tendencies of the communist view of reality as manifest in Bucharest.

Notes

1. Ihab Hassan, *Radical Innocence: The Contemporary American Novel*, New Jersey: Princeton Uni. Press, 1961, p. 290.
2. *Dangling Man*, p. 137.
3. "Existentialism is a Humanism", Walter Kaufmann ed. *Existentialism: From Dostoevsky to Sartre*, Penguin Books Ltd., 1975, p. 368.
4. *The Myth of Sisyphus*, p. 109.
5. *The Rebel*, p. 248.
6. *The Dean's December*, Penguin Books Ltd., 1982, p. 46.
7. *Ibid.*, p. 7.
8. *Ibid.*, p. 64.
9. *Ibid.*, p. 209.
10. *Ibid.*, p. 212.
11. *Ibid.*, p. 67.
12. *Ibid.*, p. 214.
13. *Ibid.*, p. 186.
14. *Ibid.*, p. 177.
15. *Idem.*
16. *Ibid.*, p. 152.
17. *Ibid.*, p. 221.
18. *Ibid.*, p. 296.
19. *Ibid.*, pp. 305-06.
20. *Ibid.*, p. 306.

Index

A

Absurdists, 130
Abel, Darrel, 16
Allen, Mary, 114
Allsop, Kenneth, 114
American Dream of Success
    Success-myth, 76
American expansionism, i, 80
American Declaration of Independence, 87
Angry Young Men, ii, 1, 3, 130
Anti-war American Novels, vi, 96
Appolinaire Guillaume, 116
    Memelles de Tiresias, Les, 116
Arms and the Man, 96

B

Balakian, Anna, 117
Barnes, Hazel, 55
Barth, John, 112, 119
    The Floating Opera, 119-20
    The Beat Generation, iv, 113, 129
Beat literature, iv
'Be-liked', 84
Bellow, Saul, iv, 157
    The Dangling Man, 157
    The Dean's December, 157-67
Berdyaev, Nicolai A, 146
Berger, Thomas, 112, 125
    Vital Parts, 121
    Crazy in Berlin, 121
    Reinhart in Love, 121
    Little Big Man, 121
Bewley, Marius, 25, 31
Black Humour, 112, 130
Bolshevik, 117
Bradbury, Malcolm, 25, 145
Breton, Andre, 12, 115, 117
    Anthology de L humor noir, 112
    Confession Le daigreuse, 115
Browell, W.C., 16
Bryant, Jerry H, 132, 139
Buber, Martin, 65

C

Calvinist theology, 20
Cambell, Jr Howard, 110
Camus, Albert, 45, 66, 113, 117, 155, 157
    The Myth of Sisyphus, 45, 113
    The Rebel, 45, 155
Carpenter I Frederic, 16-17
Cerber, John C, 11
Chase, Richard, 21
Cohen, Dean, 132
Cohen, Sarah Blacker, 114
Comte, Augustine, 61, 149
    'religion of humanity', 149
Consumerism, 82
Cooper, James Fenimore, i, 1, 3
    The Leather Stocking Tales, 2
    Littlepage trilogy novels
    Satanstoe, 9
    The Chainbreaker, 9
    The Redskins, 9
    'anti-rent struggle', 2, 9

The Crater, i, 1-10
Cozzens, James Gould, 96

D

Dada, 112
Dadaism, 112, 114
Dadaists, 114
Darwin, Charles, V
deFord, Miriam Allen, 148
Dekker, George, 3
Demonsthenes, 163
Descrates, Rene, 48
'Cogito ergo sum'
Dickens, Charles, 76
Donleavy, James Patrick, iv, 129, 130, 140
The Ginger Man, 131, 138-39
A Singular Man, 140
Meet My Maker the Mad Molecule, 141-42
The Saddest Summer of Samuel S, 141
The Beastly Beatitudes of Balthazar B, 141-42
The Onion Eaters, 142-43
A Fairy Tale of New York, 143-44
Dostoyevsky, Fyodor M, 156
The Brothers Karamazov, 12
Duffey, Bernard, 136

E

Eliot, T.S. 31
Ellison, Ralph, v
Invisible Man, v
Emerson, Ralph Waldo, v, 144
Erskine John, 16
Exodus, 5

F

Faulkner, William, 55
Felt, Joseph B., 14
Annals of Boston, 14
Feminism, 16, 87, 94
the liberal/moderate feminism, 87
the radical feminism, 87
the socialist feminism, 87
feminist consciousness, 87
Fhilbrik, Thomas, 3
Firestone, Shulamith, 94
Dialectic of Sex, 94
Fitzgerald, F. Scot, vi, 24
The Great Gatsby, vi, 24-32
This Side of Paradise, 24
'the green light' symbology, 24
'Valley of ashes', 30
Florentine Platonists,
Ficinio Marsilo, 148
Pico della Mirandolla' 148
Pomponazzi, Pietro, 148
Fogle, Richard Harter, 16
'Fourier socialists theories", 3
Fox Dixon Ryan, 3
France, Antole, 12
Thais, 12
Frankel, Haskel, 65
Freedman, Morris, 88
Freud, Sigmond, 44
Friedman, Jay Bruce, 113
Black Humour, 113
frontierman' i
frontier Movement, i
Frost, Robert, 124
Frost's humanism, 128
"Birches", 124-30
'Poetry is a metaphor', 124
Poetry 'a clarification of life' 124-25
'a bursting unity of opposites' 124

G

Gaiser, Carolyn, 138
Geoffrey, Grigson, 119
German Romantics, 46
Godwinism, 12
Gold, Herbert, 135
Goodheart, Eugene, 117
Goodman, Mitchell, 96
    The Great Depression, 66-67
Griermer, Donald J, 113
Gross, Seymour, 12

H

Hassan, Ihab, 100, 157
Hawthorne, Nathanael, vi, ii
    The Scarlet Letter, vi,
Hawthorne's humanism, 22
Heller, Joseph, 112, 120
    Scientic humanism, 145
    Christian humanism, 145
Husserl, 46
Hutchinson, Anne, 12, 16

I

I.W.W., 51-52
    Industrial Workers of the World, 51
Iroquous tribe, i
'I-Thou', 66

J

Jaffersonian agrarian democracy, vi
James, Henry, i, 33
    The Portrait of a Lady, 33-43
Jazz Age, 24
Jazz culture, vi
Jones, James, vi, 96
    From Here to Eternity, 99-102
    The Thin Redline, 99
    Whistle, 99
Jung, Carl Gustav, 44

K

Kerouac, Jack, 137
    On the Road, 137
King Lear, 163
'Know-Nothing Bohemians', 138
Koreneva, M, VI, 96, 121
Kristeller, Paul Oskar, 148

L

LeClair, T, 133
Laurtreamont Comte De, 116
    Lundoquist, James, 107
    Catch-22,120
Hemingway, Ernest, 96
    A Farewell to Arms, 97-99
Hendine Josephine, 103, 110
Heraclitus, 73
Hersey, John, 96
Holmes, John Clellon, 133
Horatio Alger dream, 134
hipster, 135
hipsterism/American Existentialism, 13
hip Morality, 135
    Hooks, Bell, 94
    Humanism, 33, 82, 144, 153
    Classical humanism, 145
    Modern humanism, 33
    Theocentric/anthropocentric humanism, 146
Heretical humanism, 146
    Scientific humanism, 145
    Christian humanism, 145
'Husserl, 46
Hutchinson, Anne, 12

I

I.W.W., 51-52
  Industrial Wreckers of the World, 51
Iroquous tribe, i
'I-Thou', 66

J

Jaffersonian agrarian democracy, vi
James, Henry, i, 33
  The Portrait of a Lady, 33-43
Jazz Age, 24
Jazz culture, vi
Jones, James, vi, 96
  From Here to Eternity, 99-102
  The Thin Redline, 99
  Whistle, 99
Jung, Carl Gustav, 44

K

Kerouac, Jack, 135
  On the Road, 135
King Lear, 161
'Know-Nothing Bohemians', 136
Koreneva, M, VI, 96,121
Kristeller, Paul Oskar, 145

L

LeClair, T, 131
Laurtreamont Comte De, 116
Lundoquist, James, 107

M

Macbeth, 161
Macmurry, John, 45
Macquarrie, John, 48
Mailer, Norman, iv, vi, 96, 134
  The Naked and the Dead, vi
McReynolds, David, 131, 133
Malamud, Bernard, iv, 65
  The Assistant, 65-75
Maritain James
Melville, Herman, i
  Moby Dick, 12
Miller, Arthur, vi, 76
  All My Sons, vi, 76-80
  Death of a Salesman, vi, 80-86, 89
Murphy Brenda
  'natural rights doctrine', 87
O'Hara, John, 126
O'Neill, Eugene, 44
  The Hairy Ape, 44-46, 54
Orthodox morality

P

Parker, Dorothy, 127
Passos, Dos, 96-97
Percy, Walker, 112
Pilgrim Fathers, 26
Plantation-myth, v
Plato, 3
'Plato's philosopher ruler'
Podhoretz, Norman, 136
Powell, R, 96
Praag, J.P. Van, 155
Promethean individualism, 117
Puritanism, 21
Pynchon, Thomas, 112, 120
  The Gravity's Rainbow, 120
  The Crying of Lot, 49, 120

R

Read, Herbert, 45
Reisman, David, 134
Ribemont-Dessaignes, Georges, 125
Richman, Sydney, 74
Richter, Hans, 116